CRM Fundamentals

Scott Kostojohn
Mathew Johnson
Brian Paulen

Apress®

CRM Fundamentals

ISBN-13 (pbk): 978-1-4302-3590-3

ISBN-13 (electronic): 978-1-4302-3591-0

President and Publisher: Paul Manning
Lead Editor: Jeffrey Pepper
Technical Reviewer: Tom McKinnie
Editorial Board: Steve Anglin, Mark Beckner, Ewan Buckingham, Gary Cornell, Jonathan Gennick, Jonathan Hassell, Michelle Lowman, James Markham, Matthew Moodie, Jeff Olson, Jeffrey Pepper, Frank Pohlmann, Douglas Pundick, Ben Renow-Clarke, Dominic Shakeshaft, Matt Wade, Tom Welsh
Coordinating Editor: Jennifer L. Blackwell
Copy Editor: Kim Wimpsett
Compositor: Bytheway Publishing Services
Indexer: SPI Global
Artist: SPI Global
Cover Designer: Anna Ishchenko

Distributed to the book trade worldwide by Springer Science+Business Media, LLC., 233 Spring Street, 6th Floor, New York, NY 10013. Phone 1-800-SPRINGER, fax (201) 348-4505, e-mail orders-ny@springer-sbm.com, or visit www.springeronline.com.

For information on translations, please e-mail rights@apress.com, or visit www.apress.com.

Apress and friends of ED books may be purchased in bulk for academic, corporate, or promotional use. eBook versions and licenses are also available for most titles. For more information, reference our Special Bulk Sales–eBook Licensing web page at www.apress.com/bulk-sales.

Contents at a Glance

Contents

About the Authors

Scott Kostojohn, Principal

Scott acts as sales director and CRM architect for Madrona Solutions Group, a leading Seattle, Washington, CRM consulting firm. Scott leverages his significant experience with various CRM platforms to support Madrona's clients during complex implementations. Prior to joining Madrona, Scott worked for Microsoft in a variety of roles, including product strategy with the Microsoft Dynamics CRM product development team. Before that, he was a CRM consultant at Equarius (now EMC) helping clients around the country implement CRM software solutions. Scott has a bachelor's of science degree in mechanical engineering from Cornell University.

Mathew Johnson, CRM Practice Director

Mathew joined Madrona Solutions Group in 2007 and currently oversees its CRM practice. He brings a deep understanding of CRM fundamentals and their application to the marketplace, and he works with the rest of the leadership team to ensure that Madrona offers an exciting and challenging environment for its employees. Prior to joining Madrona, Mathew led and delivered business-process improvement and CRM initiatives for Acetta, often using the Microsoft Dynamics CRM and Salesforce.com product platforms. Before Acetta, he was a senior consultant at Onyx Software, implementing sales, marketing, and customer service solutions. Mathew has degrees in business administration (information systems) and communications from the University of Washington.

Brian Paulen, Principal

Brian cofounded Madrona Solutions Group in July 2005. He has overall responsibility for the firm's growing business and for managing client and partner relationships. Brian has extensive project and program management experience and is an expert in delivering strategic sales and marketing solutions on various platforms. Prior to founding Madrona, Brian directed the CRM practice at Slalom Consulting. Earlier, he was a member of the CRM team at Equarius (now EMC), working primarily with clients in the Pacific Northwest. His career began at Accenture (formerly Andersen Consulting), working out of its New York office. Brian has bachelor's of art degrees in political science and international business from Lehigh University.

About the Technical Reviewer

Tom McKinnie is an experienced CRM consultant and project manager who has held senior positions at Fortune 500 companies including Nextel Communications and Microsoft Corporation before moving into consulting. His consulting clients include a wide range of small, medium, and enterprise-level companies in the advertising, information technology, construction, and manufacturing industries. He enjoys boating and mountain biking with his family in the beautiful state of Washington.

Acknowledgments

I would like to thank my wife, Phoebe, and children, Zoe and Zachary, for giving me the time and freedom to work on this project. Even though this is my second book, it took more time than I'd ever imagined. Mathew, it was a pleasure to work with you and to see the final product. Finally, I would like to thank Scott for coordinating the entire process and owning a lion's share of the writing, and Tom for his careful review and feedback.

—Brian Paulen

I want to first thank Brian and Scott for all of their support and for undertaking the heavy lifting surrounding this book, and Tom McKinnie for his technical review. This book is entirely to their credit, and I truly appreciate their efforts. I also want to thank my wife, Heidi, for all of her support and understanding throughout my career—the long days, nights, and weekends are tough for any partner to endure, and she has handled every up and down with unbelievable grace and support. To all of the colleagues and clients who I have worked with over the years, you have helped me grow professionally, and I appreciate the amazing people that I have had the pleasure to work with. Lastly, I want to thank my family for all of their love and support throughout the years because they have truly made me who I am.

—Mathew Johnson

I want to thank my wife, Vasantha, and boys, Alex and Peter, for their support and patience over the course of the project. Also, thanks to my coauthors and friends, Brian and Mathew, for all of their hard work; Tom McKinnie, our technical reviewer, for his thoughtful comments and suggestions; and the team at Apress for their guidance.

—Scott Kostojohn

Introduction

Many of you reading this book are about to embark on the journey of implementing customer relationship management (CRM) software within your organization; some of you are completely new to CRM, while others have been through a CRM implementation with varied success. This book was written to provide business leaders and stakeholders with a practical playbook that spells out an approach for a successful CRM project and program.

People often think that success with CRM starts and ends with purchasing the current popular application in the market; however, no matter the application (even with all of its cool bells and whistles), you still need to have the hard discussions about how your organization should be structured, what customer-facing processes should look like, and how all your processes should translate into the system in such a way that you effectively leverage all of the application's great features. CRM is very easy to do poorly, and many fail to get value from their investment; in fact, when we're introduced to a new client that has an existing CRM implementation, the most common pain points we observe are caused by poor implementation of the software (not the software itself). Don't get us wrong—technology is certainly involved and will impact design considerations, and the software you choose will have certain advantages and also limitations. But the important thing to remember throughout this book is that the stakeholders involved, business process discussions, and modeling and design decisions are as important, if not more so, than the software itself.

The goal of this book is to help you understand what you are really getting into when undertaking a CRM initiative: the level of effort needed to be effective and what you can reasonably hope to accomplish with CRM. This is not a visionary "pie-in-the-sky" look at CRM programs but rather a "rubber-meets-the-road" guide meant to give you a realistic approach to create an effective CRM program. Many CRM books focus on the technical ins and outs of various systems; however, this book is technology agnostic and focuses on the business components necessary to plan, organize, and deliver value to your organization by leveraging CRM concepts. You are making a significant investment in CRM, both financially and with your organization's time, so our goal is to help you get the most out of that investment. In the end, you will have the skills and tools to properly assemble your team, plan your overall program and specific iterations, and navigate the ups and downs of a CRM project while keeping your eyes on the longer-term strategy.

We hope you enjoy this book and are able to leverage many of the techniques outlined on your way to CRM success!

CHAPTER 1

Introduction

Defining CRM

For businesses, the world is growing more and more competitive, at a relentless pace. Technological innovation lowers barriers to entry, once specialized products and services become commodities, every market is suddenly crowded. The customer experience is becoming more important to businesses as a differentiator; at the same time the customer himself grows more sophisticated, more demanding, and less loyal.

To succeed, businesses need to run more efficiently than their competition, their people must be more productive and effective, and their products and services must be more closely aligned to their customer's needs. They must make more "right" decisions, and they must make them more quickly. This high level of performance requires information – about the operations of the business, about their customers and prospective customers, and about the competition.

To address these trends, businesses have increased their focus on their customers – examining the customer perspective more often in their decision-making, adjusting business processes and their organizations to provide a better customer experience, and generally managing customer information and relationships more thoughtfully and deliberately. Software tools have emerged to support businesses in this new focus on customers and customer management. Both the business strategy of increased customer focus and the class of business applications that emerged to support it are referred to as "Customer Relationship Management" or "CRM". In this book, we'll refer to the "CRM program" to describe the people, processes, and technologies a business deploys to increase their customer focus, and the "CRM application" to describe the technology element, typically centered on a CRM software package. We'll go into the different elements of the program in detail in the next chapter.

Purpose of this Book

This book is intended as a resource for anyone charged with leading or participating in a CRM program at their organization. Our objective is to provide a solid grounding in the value of CRM, to outline the components that make up a successful CRM program, and to detail the steps required to successfully launch it. We have purposefully avoided going into depth on individual CRM applications, or the technology elements of CRM. There are a profusion of books available on the ins and outs of individual CRM applications that can help your administration team be more effective. We wanted a book to equip a non-technical executive with the information to put the pieces of a CRM program together, avoid common pitfalls, and choose an appropriate application and consulting partner to assist them.

The content is organized in roughly the sequence it will be needed. Chapter Two lays out the elements of a complete and successful CRM program, so that you understand what the moving parts are and how they fit together. Chapter Three provides guidance on building your roadmap – the plan for implementing CRM, including the goals of the program and schedule for implementation. Chapter Four covers the selection process for the right CRM application and consulting partner for your organization. Chapter 5 addresses the details of planning the implementation of your roadmap, and Chapter 6 the execution of individual CRM projects. We conclude with Chapter 7, which describes strategies for maintaining and evolving CRM.

Sources of CRM Value

Now that we have established what we mean when we say "CRM", and provided a high-level outline of the book, let's explore why a business, or for that matter any organization, might embark on such a program. What is the value of CRM?

Supporting a Data-Driven, Learning Organization

The marriage of a set of well-documented, consistently-executed processes, with a business application that supports, monitors, and reports on them provides the foundation for an agile organization that learns and evolves. This agility can help you stay one step ahead of your competition. In addition to its direct role in helping users execute business processes efficiently, the CRM application's reports and dashboards act as "instrumentation" for your organization– supporting agility by enabling you to constantly assess what is working and what is not, to test hypotheses and experiment with improvements, and then to make data-driven decisions based on the results.

Consider the following exchange with a sales executive:

CRM Consultant: Do you know why your customers buy from you?

Manager: I have some idea. They buy because of customer service, and our product is superior.

CRM Consultant: How do you know this?

Manager: From talking with some of our customers.

CRM Consultant: Do you know which of these factors is most important to which customers?

Manager: No, I suppose not.

CRM Consultant: Do you know who you lose deals to most often and why?

Manager: I have an idea, but again I don't have any empirical data to support it.

This is a fairly common interaction with an organization that has either not attempted or not succeeded with implementing a CRM program. We would get similar responses if we asked about sales pipeline visibility, sales cycle duration, lost deal analysis, or customer service inquiry data (how long do inquiries take to get resolved, how many are resolved in the first call, etc.). You have heard the old aphorism "*You can't manage what you can't measure*" – consistent processes and a sophisticated CRM application can provide the platform needed to measure and manage.

Wringing out Inefficiencies and Increasing Employee Productivity

Understanding your current processes is the first step in beginning to analyze potential improvements that can be enabled by your CRM application. Entire books are dedicated to process definition and improvement so we will not go into great detail on those topics in this book; our goal is to show how a CRM system can help create efficiencies in your processes with proper analysis and implementation.

A few examples of efficiency gains from CRM can be:

- Improve lead management by feeding leads directly from website contact forms to the appropriate sales team's work queue in CRM

- Automatically assign inbound leads to the appropriate sales rep, based on geography, category, etc. This auto-assignment gets leads in the hands of sales reps more quickly.

- Automatically escalate or re-assign service issues, based on defined criteria such as priority, issue, age, type, etc. This results in more efficient issue management and improved customer experience. Service issues can no longer "slip through the cracks".

- Alert management on big sales deals – when sales deals are above a certain revenue threshold, the CRM application can automatically alert the sales leadership team so that they have visibility to the deal and can assist the account team.

- Business intelligence elements of CRM can be used to profile leads who have been successfully converted to customers, and then score inbound leads to help sales team members prioritize their calls to focus on the leads most similar to past successful leads.

- Managing quote generation within CRM ensures sales reps create valid quotes (including necessary and compatible components/products), and ensures all reps use correct pricing and up-to-date product availability. This reduces ramp-up time for new sales team members, and slashes frequency of invalid quotes.

- Relate all interactions (phone calls, important e-mail, e-mail newsletters, trade show attendance, etc.) with customers to analyze sales drivers, win or loss reasons, repeat business, etc.

Case Study: A Sales Process Enhanced by CRM

In this organization, the sales team was utilizing Excel spreadsheets to send proposals to their clients. These spreadsheets contained product information (name, prices, dependencies) so when product changes were rolled out it was necessary to send out a new spreadsheet "template" to all of the sales people. This process included significant opportunity for error:

- Sales people could mistakenly use an outdated version of the spreadsheet

- Sales people could modify (and often did) the Excel template to suit their needs without approval from a manager, finance, product development, etc. – this can result in selling things that are not able to be fulfilled, do not comply with corporate guidelines, etc.

In order to get a picture of a sales forecast for the organization, this process also meant that sales people were responsible for entering their proposal information into a separate database. The duplicate entry was a big issue because:

- Data entry errors made forecasting difficult

- Data updated in the sales person's spreadsheet was not always updated in the forecast database

- Sales people often waited to enter their deals into the forecast database until the deals were close to closing, thus to avoid wasting effort entering deals that didn't go further. This resulted in inaccurate forecasting for the organization.

The solution was to rollout a CRM application and new forecasting processes to capture sales information. The new solution reduced data entry for the sales team, improved forecast accuracy, and included proposal generation tools that increased management control over proposals. A few other operational databases were also rolled into the CRM solution so that operations staff could benefit from sales information and collaborate better with sales for that crucial handoff post-sale.

Providing a Better Customer Experience

Providing customers with the most satisfying and effective interactions possible is an increasingly important competitive differentiator. Customers are not nearly as loyal today – they can often simply search the web and find a "better" alternative to your product or service within minutes. In addition, technology tools such as blogs, ratings sites, and social networks have increased the scale and impact of the consumer's "word-of-mouth", making positive customer experiences even more important.

Customers' expectations of what defines an acceptable interaction are continually evolving, and today include the following:

- Each representative they interact with should have access to the entire organization's past interactions with you, from purchasing to service. Customers calling in for service should not need to be transferred around just to find information from their last conversation with your organization.

- Self-service options should be available so that customers can get information or initiate basic transactions themselves, 24 hours a day, 7 days a week.

- Your organization should communicate with them via whatever mode they prefer– email, phone, text message, etc.

An easy study of how customer's expectations around interactions have changed is to consider the retail banking space. It was not too long ago that all retail banking was done inside bank branches with tellers during "banker's hours". Over time, the industry introduced one innovation after another to provide better and better experiences for customers (often reducing costs at the same time). First drive-through banking was introduced, then ATM machines, and then internet banking. Somewhere along the line banks began opening for longer hours to make them more convenient. And now there are several banks that let you transact via your mobile phone, and will send you balance updates via text messages.

CRM programs support your organization's effort to meet these expectations in a number of ways:

- The evaluation of business processes from the customer perspective associated with a CRM program can result in changes that improve customer satisfaction.

- The CRM application serves as a central hub of customer information, shared by all customer-facing employees, helping them each present an informed face to the customer.

- The CRM application workflow automation can provide a platform to send communications to customers automatically based on events.

- The CRM application can act as the data store for a customer web portal to enable self-service.

- Data mining of the CRM application can identify products, services, and promotions that may be of interest to customers based on their profile.

Informing Business Decisions

Your CRM program provides a platform for gathering customer information, and making it easily available to business leaders for review and analysis. Decisions that were once made on anecdotal evidence, or only after lengthy and arduous data collection and aggregation, can be easily supported by relevant information from the CRM application. New insights into the organization and its customers can be gained, identifying new opportunities or competitive threats.

Some common areas where CRM data can help inform decision making include the following, with questions that might be answered in each area:

Sales forecasting

Will we likely make our revenue targets this month/quarter? How will sales be distributed across regions and product lines?

Sales management

Are my salespeople performing adequately? Are they balancing their time properly between closing deals and prospecting? How healthy is my sales pipeline? Which deals are they losing and why?

Product planning

What products are different types of customers buying? What products do they buy together? What are our major competitors for each product line, and in what situations do they win? Why do some products receive more customer service inquiries than others?

Customer service staffing

How does my issue load vary over time? How does staffing level impact my time to resolve issues? Is the number of interactions or escalations decreasing over time?

Marketing campaign planning

What lead sources have been most productive in the past? What are the profiles of successful leads? What types of marketing activities drive the most interest?

In addition to providing a static set of measures to monitor the ongoing health and performance of the business, the CRM program can play an active role in business planning.

The recent rise in usage and importance of social media tools can make CRM an even more useful platform for learning about customers and informing business decisions. As more customers share their opinions, needs, likes, and dislikes via tools such as blogs, Facebook, and Twitter, more of this data can be incorporated to enrich the profile of your customer and market stored in your CRM application. Many tools and services exist today to mine this information and incorporate it into your CRM application. In addition to this passive information-gathering role, these social media tools can also be use actively by your organization to open up new communication channels with customers, using the tools they are already using and prefer. These new channels can be used to provide updates from the company, deliver promotions, and gather feedback.

Preparing for CRM

Preparing Your Organization for Change

Preparing your organization for change prior to undertaking a new CRM initiative is an important contributor to CRM success. Change, even for the better, is often met with resistance, as people have a level of comfort with their current processes.

Thoughtful preparation can break down this resistance and help employees see the positive in the change and roll with the inevitable hiccups associated with new processes and applications. So how does one properly setup their organization for change? The main components that in our experience have proven successful include:

Data-Driven Culture

Pursuing a data-driven culture means documenting processes, gathering data on their effectiveness, making changes based on the data, and then evaluating the success of the change based on data. The entire process should be communicated to the extent feasible. This approach to change will help employees understand how situations are identified for potential change, how changes are developed, and how the effectiveness of those changes is measured. This kind of methodical approach inspires confidence that changes are not arbitrary; they are made with important business goals in mind, and they will be critically evaluated for success. The result will be an employee community more comfortable with change and more willing to support it. Obviously part of the purpose of your CRM initiate is to establish a framework for a data-driven culture – but to the extent possible fostering this culture prior to launching your CRM program will be beneficial.

Executive support

Having executive support for the implementation as a whole and specifically for the changes it will bring is imperative to a successful initiative. Executive(s) need to be involved enough to be able to guide decisions, and communicate the vision of the implementation project and its intended benefits.

Communication

Communication is important so that people know what to expect, which helps them prepare for the coming changes. It's important to start with a communication plan similar to that in Figure 1-1 that identifies who needs what information and when, how they are able to give feedback, who owns delivering the communication, and what channel will be used.

\<Project Name\>
Project Team Communication Plan

Deliverable	Information Needs	Description	Purpose	Delivery Method	Frequency	Owner	Feedback	Audience
Project status report	Document, issues, risks, important meetings/miles tones	Regular update on project status, issues, risks	Communicate regulular status of the project	E-mail	Weekly	Project Manager		Project Manager Project Sponsor Project Team
Project Team Email	\<Need\>	Regular update on project quality performance	\<Purpose\>	E-mail	Weekly	Quality Manager		Project Manager Project Sponsor Project Team Quality Manager
Issues Log	List of Issues, resolutions, owner	\<Description\>		Document Share	Weekly	Project Manager		Project Manager Project Sponsor Project Team
\<Deliverable\>	\<Need\>	\<Description\>		\<Delivery Method\>	\<Frequency\>	\<Owner\>		\<Audience\>
\<Deliverable\>	\<Need\>	\<Description\>		\<Delivery Method\>	\<Frequency\>	\<Owner\>		\<Audience\>

Figure 1-1. Sample Project Communication Plan

Training

Obviously training is a part of any technology implementation; however it is important to note that there are a few key things to consider when planning your program. Training early and often helps employees acclimate to the new technology and processes which reduces resistance.

Feedback

It is essential that people have a way to provide input into how their lives are impacted, positively or negatively, by a new technology/process. You will of course not be able to address each item of feedback (or in the way that the individual might prefer), however the very fact that it has been acknowledged, considered, and explained in a very honest way will go a long ways in having employees embrace the changes.

Recognition

Recognizing those that are properly utilizing the CRM system in the course of their responsibilities provides a positive example to others. This not only rewards the desired behavior, but it can show the benefit that those people are gaining in their job responsibilities (time, reduced data entry, etc.) Some good ways to recognize individuals include an email from the project "champion" to the team, small incentive rewards (i.e. gift cards), and special mentions in team meetings.

Chapter Summary

CRM is a strategy of increased focus on developing, maintaining, and extracting maximum value from customer relationships. Your CRM program includes people, business process, and technology components.

This book is intended to equip a non-technical business executive with the information needed to successfully plan and launch a CRM program.

There are many sources of value from a well-implemented CRM program, including improved employee productivity and efficiency, better customer experiences, increased business insight, and development of a data-driven, learning culture.

Preparing your organization to absorb change is groundwork that will make your CRM program launch more successful.

CHAPTER 2

Components of CRM Success

A successful CRM program provides the platform that helps your organization continually improve and refine the way it acquires and services customers. The increasing competitiveness of the business world rewards organizations that understand their customers and that can react quickly to seize opportunities and address challenges.

It's important to emphasize our use of the term *program*; success with CRM requires much more than just purchasing a CRM application and installing it. The heart of a CRM program is the continual examination and evolution of your customer interactions in order to provide better customer experiences and help your organization achieve its customer-related goals. The CRM application itself is simply the tool used to deliver great customer experiences, streamline your customer-facing operations, and gain insight into your customers and business.

Success with a CRM program is built on four pillars: having the right *people* in the organization engaged in the right roles in the CRM program, implementing well-designed internal and customer-facing *processes*, implementing the right supporting *technology*, and setting reasonable *expectations* for what success looks like and what kind of effort and cost are required to achieve it. Let's consider each component in turn.

People

Your CRM program will require a number of people from different parts of the organization playing different roles. Job titles and requirements will depend on the organization, but for most organizations, the following roles should be assigned for a successful CRM implementation.

Executive Sponsor

The executive sponsor is the senior executive who is ultimately accountable for the success of the CRM program within your organization and is responsible for the following:

- Securing necessary funding for the CRM program.

- Guiding the ongoing CRM roadmap development process to ensure that the roadmap is well aligned with the organization's strategic goals. Roadmap development is described in detail in Chapter 3.

- Ensuring engagement at the executive level from the different groups within the organization that need to contribute to the CRM program.

- Setting goals for the CRM program and holding individuals and teams accountable.

- Being the ultimate decision maker for CRM questions within the organization.

Important qualifications for a CRM executive sponsor include the following:

- Must be a CRM "believer." His or her tone, engagement level, and enthusiasm all have an outsized influence on the CRM program.

- Should be experienced with the people and processes in the customer-facing part of the organization. A finance or IT executive is not the ideal person for this role.

Employees follow their leaders; the executive sponsor's frequent, vocal, enthusiastic focus on CRM will communicate to the entire organization that CRM is part of its "DNA" and that each employee needs to make sure it is given priority. In addition to this evangelism, executives also need to hold each layer of management accountable for the success of CRM in their departments.

Steering Committee

The steering committee is the critical body for guiding the CRM program within your organization. It should be chaired by your executive sponsor and include representatives from all the key CRM constituent groups (for example, inside sales, field sales, customer service, and marketing) as well as from IT and from the CRM administration team (described in a moment). The committee should meet regularly; your situation will dictate the appropriate frequency.

The steering committee's responsibilities include the following:

- Managing the ongoing change control process for production CRM applications. This is the formal evaluation and approval process for configuration changes to the CRM application, used once CRM is in production to ensure that proposed changes do not interfere with any group's usage of CRM and that they are aligned with the overall CRM roadmap and to communicate these changes to the various CRM constituencies. Developing and implementing a change control process is described in Chapter 6.

- Developing and maintaining the CRM roadmap for the organization. The roadmap describes the plan for enhancing the CRM program over time and how these enhancements support the organization's strategic goals. The roadmap may describe new capabilities to be added to CRM, new user groups to be migrated to the application, or new business processes to be implemented and supported with CRM. Roadmap development is covered in detail in Chapter 3.

- Planning budget requirements for CRM, based on the roadmap.

Important qualifications for CRM steering committee members include the following:

- They can accurately represent the needs of their constituency to the steering committee.

- They can understand how changes to the CRM program raised in the steering committee will impact their constituency.

- They can dedicate the time needed to participate fully in the activities of the committee.

The IT representative can help inform the committee of planned IT initiatives that may impact the CRM program, as well as coordinate the support provided by the IT organization for the CRM application. This role is less critical for software-as-a-service applications, because the IT department's responsibility for these applications is typically small or nonexistent, and it is more critical for on-premises CRM applications.

The CRM administration team manages the execution of the CRM roadmap, the enhancement of the CRM application, and the training and support of users. They are typically the application experts and can help identify how the application can be used to help achieve a business goal identified by the steering committee.

Implementation Team

The composition of the implementation team, charged with the initial rollout of your CRM program, will vary according to the complexity of your organization and the initial implementation project. In this section, we'll describe the key roles on the implementation team; in many cases, a single individual may play multiple roles.

Executive Sponsor

The role of the sponsor was described earlier, and as for the overall CRM program, this person is also responsible for the success of the initial implementation. Typically the sponsor will want to stay current on the status and progress of the project and assist the implementation team by clearing bureaucratic obstacles and encouraging engagement across the company to help support the success of the implementation.

Project Manager

The initial CRM implementation is a complex undertaking, requiring input from numerous departments and potentially changing behaviors and processes for all of the organization's customer-facing employees. A dedicated project manager is key to plan the project, keep it on schedule, and maintain communication throughout.

Subject-Matter Experts

The subject-matter experts (SMEs) are the individuals on the team with a deep understanding of the business areas that will be impacted by CRM and will help guide the process design and CRM application design to meet the project goals. For a sales-focused project, for example, the SME team might include the director of sales, an experienced field sales representative, and an experienced inside-sales representative. It is important that the SMEs understand the situation "on the ground" today (what the current processes and what tools are being used) as well as the larger picture - the longer-term organization vision for CRM in their area, and the immediate project goals that help achieve the vision.

Some organizations have a tendency to want to leave the individual user/contributor (for example, the salesperson in the earlier example) out of the process, either because of fears of losing their productivity by taking their time with the project or because of fears that they can't think "big picture" enough to contribute. In our experience, this is a serious risk. Oftentimes, especially in larger organizations, executives do not have a sufficient grasp of how things actually work at the lower levels of the organization, where customer interactions actually occur. If they provide the only voice to inform the process and application design, you may end up with a gap between today's process and tools and the new CRM solution that is too broad to be bridged.

IT Representative

Typically the rollout of a CRM program includes a significant technology component: a new CRM application, a set of modifications to an existing CRM application, new application integrations to streamline operations, or new reporting and analytics tools. For this reason, it's important to include the IT department on the project team. Their responsibility on the project may be to procure and maintain server hardware, update client machines, assist the consulting team with network and server access, and potentially do some development and testing work. For on-premises deployments, the IT organization will also be responsible for disaster recovery planning and application backup.

User Trainers

A significant component of the initial CRM implementation project is user training. Trainers on the project team need to communicate to users how their work processes are changing as part of the project and how the new technology tools should be used to support these new processes. Some organizations have dedicated training departments, and others pull their trainers from the departments being trained; often the SMEs on the implementation team end up playing the role of trainer for their groups.

Departmental Champions

"Champions" are the point people within each group of employees impacted by CRM. Typically they have received additional training and potentially been involved in the design process and are charged with helping drive the success and adoption of the CRM processes and tools in their groups. Champions act as first-line user support for the CRM application and for the CRM-related process and as the eyes and ears of the CRM implementation team postlaunch to spot friction points and issues. They also have a key role to play in "evangelizing" the new processes and tools.

Consulting Partner Team

If you have engaged a consulting partner to assist you, their project lead and project consultants will have key roles to play during the implementation. Typically the partner project lead and your organization's project manager will work hand in hand to manage the project.

15

Departmental Champions

The champions, described briefly earlier, are a set of individuals working within the groups of the organization involved in customer processes who act as an ongoing conduit between the group and the CRM steering committee and CRM administration teams.

These champions add tremendous value in the following ways to your CRM program:

- Help with training and mentorship of employees, including communicating best practices around the use of the CRM application

- Communicate process and application feedback from employees in their group to the CRM steering committee and/or administration team

- Be vocal supporters of CRM; for this reason, it is useful to select people who are perceived as leaders in their departments

Champions act as the CRM program's "eyes and ears" within their department. They see how the application is actually used in practice by customer-facing employees and therefore what is working well and what is not working well. They are a great source of process and application improvement ideas and can alert the larger CRM team when plans are being made based on faulty assumptions of how processes work. They also play an important role in preparing their departments for process and application changes.

The CRM Administration Team

The CRM administration team is charged with two missions. The first is the ongoing, regular maintenance of the CRM program; this includes a variety of tasks, such as the following:

- Providing end-user support for the CRM application. Sometimes there is a centralized help desk within the IT department that may provide basic, "tier-one" support, but even in these situations, the CRM administration team has a support role to play as an escalation point for more complex issues. There may also be regular tasks that are more complex and that users require assistance with, such as data loads, mass e-mails, and complex queries.

- Maintaining the health of the CRM application. Again, depending on the structure of your IT organization, some tasks may be handled outside the CRM administration team, but they include applying software updates to the CRM application and the underlying operating system and database software, ensuring that the application is being backed up regularly both on-site and off-site, and preparing and practicing for disaster recovery. These tasks are not needed if you are using a software-as-a-service application.

- Administering users within the CRM application, including creating accounts for new employees, deactivating departing employees, and adjusting security access as employees move between groups or change roles.

The second mission is to identify, plan, and implement enhancements to the CRM processes and application. These enhancements may be identified by users and addressed as part of the regular CRM change control process outlined in Chapter 6, or they may be part of the CRM roadmap. The CRM roadmap is the phased plan for the development of the CRM program, which is always evolving. How to develop and maintain a CRM roadmap is covered in the next chapter. These enhancements can range from relatively minor in scope (adding fields to an object in the CRM application or automating an e-mail communication to smooth a transition from one team to another in a process) or significant such as bringing a new department into the CRM program.

Some of the following roles may be held by members of the IT department. If not, especially if your CRM application is hosted by your own company, there should be some representation from the IT department on the CRM administration team, even if it is simply as "virtual" team members who are kept in the loop about the work of the CRM administration team.

CRM Program Lead

The CRM program lead is the overall project manager and orchestrator for the CRM program. This individual manages both the regular maintenance of CRM, as well as the enhancement processes (regular change control and roadmap execution). Key skills of this individual include the following:

- Strong project management skills

- Understanding of customer-facing part of the organization and empathy for customer-facing employees

- Ability to communicate comfortably at the executive level

- Experience with managing technology systems, vendors, and software developers

CRM Business Analyst

The role of the CRM business analyst is to combine three strands of understanding to help define a future state in which the organization is more effective and achieving its business goals. The first understanding is how employees work today, the second is what the organization's CRM goals are, and the third is a deep understanding of how the CRM application can be configured and customized. Combining these, the business analyst can outline how a given work process and the supporting CRM application can be modified to make the organization more successful.

Key skills of the CRM business analyst include the following:

- Experience with process design/reengineering

- Experience with requirements gathering for technology systems

- Experience developing functional specifications for software applications

- Deep understanding of and experience with your chosen CRM application

- Deep understanding of the business processes supported by your CRM application

CRM Administrator

The CRM administrator is the central figure in maintaining and modifying the CRM application and, with the exception of the CRM developer described next, is typically the most technical member of the CRM administration team. This individual handles user support issues, maintains the application health, handles user management, and makes configuration changes as needed. In addition, this person typically manages data imports and the installation of any product add-ons.

Key skills of the CRM administrator include the following:

- Experience administering an enterprise database-based application (required for on-premises CRM only)

- Deep understanding of and experience with your chosen CRM application

CRM Developer

Most CRM applications can be modified in limited ways via a set of configuration tools that do not require deep technical skills. However, in most cases, implementing custom business logic to support your organization's specific business processes, building integrations to other applications, or developing highly customized reports all require programming. For this reason, organizations with significant complexity should consider having a software developer on the CRM administration team.

The specific skills and experience needed will be determined by your organization's choice of CRM application.

CRM Trainer

Training is an ongoing process within your CRM program. New employees join the organization, and enhancements to both CRM processes and applications necessitate ongoing training for existing employees. Typically this training is handled within the department, often by the departmental champions described earlier. However, larger organizations may include a trainer as part of the CRM administration team. These dedicated trainers collaborate with the departmental champions to develop training materials and curriculum. Significant application or process changes may also require the CRM administration team to step in and provide training to employees rather than have training handled within the department.

Tailoring the People to Your Organization

"Roles" may have been a better word for this section than "People." We have outlined the set of roles that are needed to make a CRM program successful. How these roles will be filled by people depends greatly on your organization and the scope of your CRM program. A couple of examples may be instructive:

Example 1:

Consider a small business using CRM to bring efficiency and visibility to its sales department.

CRM administrator/CRM trainer: Susan (IT)

CRM executive sponsor: Albert (president)

Sales department champion/CRM program lead/CRM business analyst: Jane (director of sales)

Steering committee: Albert, Jane, Susan

In this example, Susan handles all the technical tasks associated with the CRM application: support, maintenance, user management, and configuration. Jane is the driver of the CRM program; she manages the CRM roadmap, makes sure the sales staff is adopting the processes and application, and looks for new opportunities to use CRM to solve business problems and to improve customer processes. Albert acts as the executive sponsor; he works with Jane on budget issues, negotiates with CRM vendors, and so on. The team has no development skills and looks to outside consultants when development is needed.

Example 2:

Consider a large organization with global employee base using CRM processes and applications across their large sales and small customer service departments.

> *CRM administrator*: Peter (application analyst)

> *CRM developer*: Arthur (application developer)

> CRM program lead/CRM business analyst: Diane (sales operations manager)

> *CRM executive sponsor*: Leslie (chief operating officer)

> *Sales department champions*: Tom (inside-sales director), Anne (field account executive, United States), Richard (field account executive, United Kingdom), Lisa (regional sales manager, LATAM)

> *Customer service department champion*: Earl (customer service representative)

> *Steering committee*: Leslie, Diane, Frank (VP of sales), Jill (VP of customer service), Robin (director of IT), Phillip (VP of marketing)

The larger organization in this example demands a larger team. Technical tasks are divided between Peter and Arthur. Diane is the overall program driver; her sales operations background is an important asset in understanding how the sales team works and how best to improve. The larger organization means a larger set of champions to ensure good representative and coverage of the customer-facing employees. With a developer on staff (Arthur), the organization is relatively self-sufficient and does not typically engage outside consulting partners.

These two examples highlight a few important guidelines when mapping people in your organization to CRM program roles:

- Ensure that the steering committee includes representation from all customer-facing departments. Note in Example 2, even though the organization is using the CRM applications in the sales and customer service departments only at this time, a marketing department executive is on the steering committee.

- For organizations with geographically dispersed employees, make sure the different regions have representation in the CRM program. Without this, employees in some areas may feel that processes and applications that are not suitable for them are being forced on them and that they do not have a voice in the process. Note in Example 2 the sales department champions are drawn from various regions.

- One role per person is the exception, not the rule, especially in smaller organizations. In Example 1, Jane is central to the program and is responsible for several different roles. How roles are spread across your team will depend on each individual's skills, experience, and interests, as well as the nature and scope of your program.

Process

We will address the topic of CRM processes in two parts. The first part will discuss the operational processes that your organization has implemented within your customer-facing departments. These are always a focus of CRM programs; organizations embark on CRM programs to produce a set of customer-related outcomes, and the CRM program improves or reinvents their business processes to achieve these outcomes. The second part will review the new processes to be put into place to manage the CRM program itself, specifically, ongoing maintenance and enhancement processes.

Operational Processes

Every organization and its processes are unique, which prevents us from offering specific templates or guidance for what your own operational processes should look like or what changes should be made. However, in our experience, assisting clients in establishing and executing CRM programs, we have observed and can describe common categories of process improvement that appear over and over again as objectives of CRM programs.

Provide Metrics and Visibility to Customer Operations

Many organizations lack a well-designed approach to recording information about customer interactions in such a way that the information is broadly visible and actionable. Everything is handled in e-mail or in monthly reports that are arduously created, reviewed once, and then tossed into a folder somewhere. There is no platform for systematic information gathering. Running an organization of any size this way is analogous to flying a plane without any instruments. You are operating on anecdote and "feel" and have little ability to forecast the future or learn from the past. There is no way to judge the impact of procedure changes or new investments. Just as you can fly an airplane more effectively with a set of instruments that provide information on how the aircraft is performing, you can manage your organization more effectively if it too is "instrumented." CRM applications can be thought of as a way to implement an instrumentation platform for your customer-facing processes that allows you to define key metrics and then capture the data to provide this metric as part of your business processes. This ability to drive metrics and gain visibility into operations is an important motivation for many organizations to embark on CRM programs.

A simple example may help ground some of this theoretical discussion of metrics and process:

Consider an organization weighing an investment in a vertical marketing. Unfortunately, the organization has only anecdotal information about its customers' market sectors and therefore no quantitative understanding of what markets to target and what products to emphasize in each market.

Recognizing this, the CRM team makes the following adjustments:

1. It creates an attribute in the CRM application to categorize customers and prospects by market sector.

2. It modifies the inside sales team's qualification process to include capturing a prospect's market sector and entering the information into CRM.

3. It asks the account manager team to update CRM and enter the market sector for each of their customers.

4. It modifies the customer service team's issue creation process to include a check to see whether CRM contains the customer's market sector and, if not, to collect it.

5. It creates a report that breaks down customers, prospects, and opportunities by market sector and illustrates the average deal size and product mix in each market sector.

After 60 days, the report provides actionable insight into which markets drive the most revenue for the organization and which products are most successful in each market sector. This information allows the marketing team to craft a vertical marketing strategy with a maximum chance for success.

This example highlights the power of CRM to "instrument" the organization and collect information to answer meaningful business data—through a combination of people, processes, and technology.

Improve Customer "Handoffs" Between Departments

Botched customer handoffs are all too common and can result in lost revenue and a poor customer experience. Two examples highlight what we mean by a poor handoff:

> Example 1: Passing a qualified sales lead from inside sales/marketing to a field sales representative
>
> In many organizations, initial lead qualification is completed by the marketing or inside-sales departments; only well-qualified leads are passed to the field sales team. Often this handoff is accomplished over e-mail, and there are many ways that this can be botched; if the field sales rep is on vacation, is having e-mail problems, or simply overlooks the e-mail, the lead can get dropped. The inside-sales person has no visibility into what has happened to it after handing it off.
>
> Example 2: Escalating a support issue
>
> Large support organizations are often segmented into tiers; issues are funneled through increasingly experienced and specialized support representatives to make the best use of each individual's capabilities. In this model, a customer may end up speaking with two or three different representatives to work an issue through to resolution. In many situations, this hand-off from one representative to the next tier is a "cold" one, meaning the new rep receives no context about the issue before interacting with the customer, forcing them to explain their issue from the beginning to each successive representative. This is a frustrating and inefficient process for the customer.

CRM applications can potentially improve the handoffs in your organization.

- Example 1: CRM workflow automation can keep items from "falling through the cracks." Following a handoff, a certain period of inactivity can trigger a reassignment or e-mail notification.

- Example 2: Having your customer-facing employees all working in the same CRM application makes it simpler to pass context with the handoff to ensure that the experience is as seamless as possible for the customer or prospect.

Implement and Enforce Structured Sales Methodology

CRM applications are ideally suited to helping implement a structured sales methodology. These methodologies include proven best practices, and CRM applications can guide salespeople to help them execute the methodology consistently. In addition, CRM can provide visibility to sales management of how well salespeople are following the methodology and how it is impacting sales performance. Detailed CRM analytics can help the organization customize and tune the methodology to further increase performance.

Focus Marketing Spending

A typical challenge of marketing groups is to understand the revenue impact of their marketing spend so that they can allocate funds to programs that produce results and eliminate programs that do not. Disconnected marketing and sales systems prevent many organizations from being able to even catalog the marketing touches received by a given prospect that was successfully converted to a customer.

CRM applications not only can close the loop between sales and marketing teams, but they can be used to test different marketing approaches (for example, different direct mail pieces or list sources) and measure the result through the sales cycle.

Target Marketing Touches

For organizations whose customer information is spread across a number of systems, targeting customers and prospects for specific marketing messages, based on their purchase history, order volume, geography, web site activity, and so on, can be a prohibitively difficult data management task. Not only must the data all be brought together in a single environment for filtering, but a customer ID table must be developed and maintained to know that Account #245 in the accounting system is the same entity as Customer #8879 in the marketing database is the same entity as Visitor #98786 in the web site tracking application.

Centralizing customer information in a CRM application and building thoughtful integrations to other key applications such as accounting and your web site can facilitate this task. Having all the needed criteria for filtering and targeting marketing touches within CRM allows for more personalized marketing without a complex data manipulation effort to combine data from disparate applications.

Enable Customer Self-Service

Customer self-service is a rare initiative that offers the promise of simultaneously decreasing service costs and increasing customer satisfaction. A healthy self-service channel allows an organization to serve the same customer base with fewer customer service staff and offers the customer a faster, more efficient service experience. For organizations with basic customer service tools, self-service is one of three common focus areas for CRM programs, the other two being the implementation of structured issue tracking and the development of a searchable knowledge base tool. Typically self-service is the third of these areas to be developed; first an organization wants to streamline its internal processes around issue management and seed its knowledge base and only then offer customers self-service options.

The most common way customer self-service is addressed within CRM programs is the deployment of a customer web portal. This is a secure web site where customers can log in and interact directly with the CRM application in a controlled manner, without the need for a customer service representative to assist them. Common tasks undertaken by customers within a customer web portal include searching the knowledge base for resolutions to issues; creating, viewing, or updating existing service issues; downloading support materials such as manuals and datasheets; and updating their profile information (addresses, phone numbers, and so on).

Manage Service Escalations

Hand in hand with implementing the structured customer service issue management processes that are often part of a CRM program are the development of policies around service escalations. Well-designed service departments and escalation policies can help strike a balance between providing a positive customer experience and controlling services costs and are especially critical for organizations for which required response and resolution times are spelled out in their customer contracts.

The robust workflow logic available in today's CRM applications facilitates compliance with escalation policies and can automate the assignment of issues within the service group and the related communications both within the group and with customers.

Analytics

Many organizations find themselves again and again forced to make important business decisions without the benefit of solid customer data. They find either that they are not collecting the information that they need or that it is collected but is spread across so many groups and applications that it cannot be synthesized in a reasonable time or at a reasonable cost.

CRM applications can help in that they centralize customer information in a single place and include robust querying and reporting tools for analysis. For more complex needs, a fuller business intelligence program may be needed, for which CRM would be one data source of perhaps many, including financial accounting applications, service scheduling applications, or provisioning applications.

We encourage all organizations initiating a CRM program to include some focus on reporting and analytics. These are the primary ways that managers and executives interact with and realize value from the CRM application, and if these stakeholder groups are not satisfied with CRM, their engagement will suffer and jeopardize the success of the program.

CRM Maintenance Processes

While the prior section highlighted some common business process areas that organizations target for improvement as part of their CRM programs, this section will introduce the processes needed to maintain and evolve your CRM program. These CRM maintenance processes are covered in greater detail in Chapters 3 and 6.

Support

CRM program support for employees can be broken out into business process support, CRM application support, and the intersection of the two.

Because the CRM program often includes redesigning customer-facing processes, the CRM team needs to be prepared to support employees with questions about the process steps and how to handle exceptions. Good documentation and training play obvious roles, but there will always be a need for process support.

CRM application support is like technical support for any business application: users have problems with the software, encounter error messages, or simply forget how to accomplish tasks within the application.

The intersection of these two categories of support is often neglected in training and documentation. As an example, you can train a user how to qualify a lead in the CRM application, but this is insufficient; they must also understand at what point in the process a lead is considered "qualified" and the actions that should be taken. The sales process may proscribe a set of customer meetings, and the CRM application training shows how to record a customer meeting, but should *all* customer meetings be entered into the CRM application? If not, which ones should be? What information must be entered for them? This explanation of how the CRM application should be used in the context of the business process is often omitted in CRM training.

Training

Training is an ongoing component of your CRM program. As new employees join the organization, they need to be trained both on your customer-facing processes as well as on the use of the CRM application to support them. Existing employees need to receive additional training as processes are refined and enhancements are made to the application or when new software versions introduce significant changes. The administration team also benefits from regular application training, especially as new software versions are released.

Most training, couched as it is in business process, is developed and delivered within an employee's group, but the CRM administration team may have a role to play in generic application training.

We have seen a number of training formats successfully used for CRM training, including traditional classroom style, webinar, and self-paced online training. Some clients have also created short video recordings of common application actions that can be accessed by users on an internal web site.

Technology Maintenance and Disaster Recovery

On-premises CRM applications, like any enterprise software, have a set of processes needed to support them, including data backup and disaster recovery, software patching, periodic hardware upgrades, and so on. The details of these processes are outside the scope of this book.

CRM applications offered as a software-as-a-service do not require these processes.

CRM Enhancement Processes

Two processes, executing in parallel, are responsible for the evolution and enhancement of your CRM program. The first is an ongoing change control process, which addresses minor and ad hoc changes and enhancements to either the CRM processes or technology. The second is a more involved roadmap development and execution process, which ensures that the CRM program continues to support the strategic objectives of the organization and is used to plan and manage major program changes. We'll describe each of these processes in this section.

Change Control

For them to be effective, CRM programs must span your organization and touch all of your customer-facing groups in some form. Customer processes cross groups, and the CRM application is generally the hub that is shared by all employees across groups to record customer interactions. Because of this interconnectedness, changes to the CRM program can have broad impact and must be controlled; if each group could independently make changes as they saw fit without consulting or communicating with the other groups, confusion and chaos could result. A well-designed change control process prevents this and includes the following:

- A system for capturing and cataloguing proposed changes to CRM processes or the CRM application from all groups involved in the CRM program

- A standing meeting to review, discuss, and approve/defer/reject proposed changes

- Regular communication to the CRM community within the organization to inform them of proposed/approved/rejected changes and the implementation schedule for approved changes

- An ongoing minor release schedule into which changes to the CRM application can be funneled for detailed design, development, test, and deployment

Running in parallel to this ongoing change control process is the roadmap development and execution process, which drives major planned changes to the CRM program.

Roadmap Development and Execution

The CRM roadmap is the longer-term plan for the CRM program, used to manage significant enhancements and, more importantly, to ensure that the CRM program is aligned with the organization's strategic business goals. The roadmap defines the major CRM initiatives for the upcoming one to two years and is informed by the organizations plans.

There are two primary roadmap processes. The first is its ongoing development. The roadmap needs to be continually developed to always reflect the plans for the next two years. This requires engagement with an organization's senior leadership, as well as the CRM executive sponsor and steering committee. The second process is the actual execution of the CRM plans.

Roadmap initiatives may involve any part of the CRM program, including the people, business processes, and CRM applications. Following, we have included a sample roadmap for a fictional company, ABC Industries, a high-tech equipment manufacturer. ABC Industries has recently launched a CRM program and rolled out a new CRM application in the sales organization with plans to phase it in companywide.

Sample CRM Roadmap: ABC Industries

2011 Q1	Map out sales business process for new product
	Plan and execute CRM application enhancements to support new product
	Execute process and application training for the new product sales team
Q2	Review e-mail communication strategies
	Roll out the integrated e-mail marketing solution
Q3	Upgrade the CRM application version

Q4   Review and revise issue management processes as needed

               Implement CRM applications for issue management in customer service and tech support

2012 Q1   Implement CRM application for issue management in customer service and tech support (continued)

Q2   Integrate web site traffic and behavior tracking into the CRM application

Q3   Review and revise the sales territory strategy

               Implement personnel and process changes

               Implement associated CRM application changes

Q4   Design and implement a customer self-service portal

An important point to remember regarding roadmaps is that they are "living" plans, and subject to constant revision. They intend to represent the current plan for the CRM program but must change as circumstances and organization goals change.

Technology

For many, CRM *is* a technology and nothing more. If you were one of those people, ideally you are beginning to realize that the technology is one piece of the puzzle; it is the tool, the enabler. But it must be developed in concert with your organizational model and business processes to be successful. In this section, we will focus on providing an overview of CRM applications and technology. We will take a deeper look in Chapter 4 at how to choose a CRM application that suits your organization.

CRM Application Infrastructure Overview

At its heart, the CRM application is a database with which users interact via an application server, using a variety of different clients. Figure 2-1 provides an overview of a typical CRM application technology architecture.

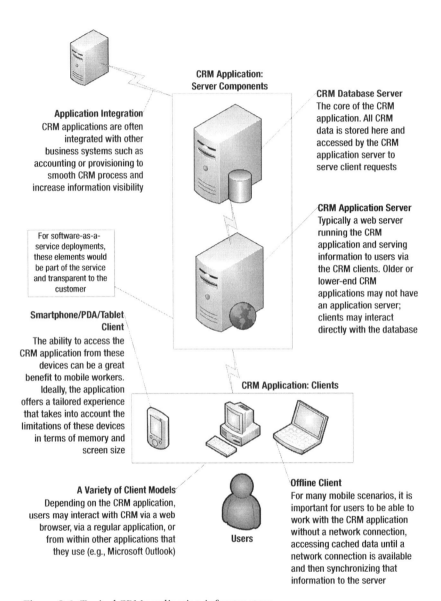

Application Integration
CRM applications are often integrated with other business systems such as accounting or provisioning to smooth CRM process and increase information visibility

**CRM Application:
Server Components**

CRM Database Server
The core of the CRM application. All CRM data is stored here and accessed by the CRM application server to serve client requests

For software-as-a-service deployments, these elements would be part of the service and transparent to the customer

CRM Application Server
Typically a web server running the CRM application and serving information to users via the CRM clients. Older or lower-end CRM applications may not have an application server; clients may interact directly with the database

Smartphone/PDA/Tablet Client
The ability to access the CRM application from these devices can be a great benefit to mobile workers. Ideally, the application offers a tailored experience that takes into account the limitations of these devices in terms of memory and screen size

CRM Application: Clients

A Variety of Client Models
Depending on the CRM application, users may interact with CRM via a web browser, via a regular application, or from within other applications that they use (e.g., Microsoft Outlook)

Users

Offline Client
For many mobile scenarios, it is important for users to be able to work with the CRM application without a network connection, accessing cached data until a network connection is available and then synchronizing that information to the server

Figure 2-1. Typical CRM application infrastructure

The complexity of your CRM infrastructure will mirror the scale of your organization. Small CRM implementations may make do with a single physical server playing the roles of both application and database server. Enterprise CRM deployments may have many servers to spread the load of large numbers of users and to provide redundancy to avoid system downtime, and their environment may include other hardware components such as network load balancers and dedicated storage appliances. Your consulting partner and IT team should work together to predict the CRM application usage in your environment and size your infrastructure accordingly. Consider your roadmap when making infrastructure decisions; if you scale your hardware to match your pilot user load, you may be very unhappy when you roll out the application to a much larger user community for production usage.

As part of the general trend in the technology industry toward cloud computing, most of the leading CRM application vendors now offer their products as a "software-as-a-service" or "cloud" application. In this model, the server components outlined in Figure 2-1 are owned and managed by the vendor, transparently. The application is purchased on a subscription basis and accessed over the Internet. If the application is accessed via a web browser, the customer does not need to install any software. The choice of deployment model (traditional on-premises vs. software-as-a-service) should be driven by a number of factors, including long-term cost, availability of IT support resources, sensitivity of the data to be stored, required level of customization and integration, and so on.

Production, Development, and Testing Environments

In addition to your production CRM application deployment, you will likely want to operate one or more additional CRM application deployments for development, testing, or training purposes.

Potentially as part of your initial CRM launch or down the road as your requirements mature, you may find the need to develop custom components for your CRM application, perhaps to add new features or to integrate with other business systems in your organization. Developing custom components inside your production environment is fraught with risk, and we strenuously advise against it. It can be disruptive to the production users, may cause system downtime or interruption, and may corrupt data.

Thorough testing is important to ensure that new custom components function as designed and that no existing functionality or processes are negatively impacted. Ideally, a third CRM environment, specifically for testing, would be used. This environment should match the production environment as closely as possible, with respect to hardware, software infrastructure versions, and so on, to provide a high level of confidence that custom components that perform well in testing will also perform once migrated to your production environment. Separating development and testing into separate environments is important; for any significant size of development effort, these two activities cannot really happen in the same environment. Testers need a stable, consistent environment running a known set of code to do their work. They can't function if developers are constantly injecting newly written code into the system.

Larger organizations have a significant ongoing training need, and many will set up separate environments for this purpose. We have also seen testing and training share environments, but this can be confusing for trainees because they may see new feature work under development that does not yet exist in the production environment.

However many environments you intend to manage as part of your CRM program, it is time well spent to map out the steps for two important processes:

- Refresh development/test from production: Periodically, perhaps between development projects, you will want to sync your development and test environments with production so that they are again replicas of production. This ensures that these environments are not slowly drifting away from production, and it brings fresh data into the environments to assist in development and testing. The process should be well-documented, repeatable, and ideally not too onerous. Privacy policies may require some data from production (for example, Social Security numbers) or be omitted or obfuscated in development and test environments.

- Migrate custom components from development to test to production: It is valuable to document both the "process" and "technical" steps to migrate custom components from development to test to production. The process steps will likely be defined as part of your development methodology, with prescribed gates and quality bars for each environment. The "technical" steps to migrate custom components will vary depending on your CRM application.

Note that these processes may be significantly different depending on how your CRM application is deployed (hosted on the premises or via software-as-a-service), but regardless of your deployment model, the need for nonproduction environments and the ability to execute these two processes both exist.

Source Control

Most CRM deployments can benefit from and ought to be using some form of source-code control to manage configurations and custom components. The advantages of using source control are great, and the overhead is not nearly as significant as you might imagine. Managing any development effort with more than one developer will quickly break down without it. For nondevelopers, source-code control systems manage the source code for configurations and custom components (typically dozens to hundreds of small files) and provide the following benefits:

- Help prevent or manage collisions where different developers independently make changes to the same files

- Allow access to a history of file changes and reversion back to prior versions of files as needed

- Allow multiple versions of the software to be run to allow for branched development and help isolate bugs

There are several options for source-code control from a number of vendors, including some robust, no-cost, open source applications.

Common CRM Application Functionality

As an introduction to the CRM application space, in this section we'll outline common functionality found in leading CRM applications. This will provide a framework that will help you understand and evaluate different applications more quickly and effectively.

Customers

Customer records are the heart of the CRM application, around which most other information revolves. These are broken into "account" or "company" records to represent organizations that you interact with, and "contact" or "individual" records to represent individuals.

Key customer functionality to look for includes the following:

- The ability to add fields to categorize customers in multiple ways— by sales territory, by market segment, or by industry

- The ability to track multiple types of organizations, either using the customer record or using other records, such as partners, vendors, and prospects

- The ability to create multiple, ad hoc relationships to link accounts and contacts in order to represent the multitude of important relationships that might exist

- The ability to easily track interactions with customers such as meetings, phone calls, e-mails, and faxes

33

Marketing

Marketing features are intended to help execute and track outbound marketing activity such as direct mail, e-mail blasts, and telesales call-downs. A critical factor is how well the marketing thread is persisted through to the sales area, to help tie revenues to marketing activities. This is a common challenge for marketing teams and one that CRM applications are well-suited to address.

Key marketing functionality to look for includes the following:

- The ability to manage suspect/prospect information independently from customers for qualification and marketing purposes

- The ability to develop lists using various criteria and then direct marketing activities against the lists

- The ability to organize marketing activities into campaigns for planning purposes

- The ability to execute direct e-mail campaigns in a robust way (for example, tracking e-mail opens, bounces, and forwards; using rich templates for e-mails; and managing the opt-in/opt-out process)

- The ability to tie sales and customer acquisition activity back to marketing efforts

Sales

The sales department is where CRM applications got their start (referred to as sales force automation [SFA] applications in the early days), and sales teams continue to be the primary driver for CRM initiatives. There are a number of motivations for bringing CRM applications and well-designed CRM processes to sales teams—the most popular include providing management with better visibility to sales activity and the sales pipeline, helping to support a structured sales methodology, and reducing administrative work and helping salespeople be more productive.

Key sales functionality to look for includes the following:

- The ability to manage sales opportunity information such as deal size, estimate close date, products/services being sold, and stage in the sales cycle

- The ability to define and manage a structured sales methodology

- The ability to create quotes for presentations to customers and prospects

- The ability to create a sales forecast for reporting to sales management

Service

The customer service features of CRM applications are intended to help organizations record customer issues and effectively manage them through to resolution. Service processes are often among the most studied and structured in an organization, because of their significant impact on the customer experience and the desire to control costs in a department that is not traditionally a profit center.

Additional benefits of managing service processes within the CRM application include the following:

- Service staff members are often a source of potential follow-on business within existing accounts—by having service employees working in the same application as sales, handoffs between the teams can be streamlined, and workflow automation can prevent dropped leads.

- Service issue data is a rich trove of information that can be used to improve and refine the organization's products, services, and customer-facing processes. The easy linkage between service data and customer data allows for insight into the distribution of service-issue categories across customer segments.

Key service functionality to look for includes the following:

- The ability to manage and categorize service issues (often referred to as *cases* or *trouble tickets*). Information tracked for each issue may include the stage in the service process, issue type, related products/services, and issue owner.

- The ability to define and support multiple issue resolution processes for different categories of issues.

- The ability to support service queues to facilitate issue routing and resolution.

- The ability to deploy a self-service portal where customers can log in to create, update, and view service issues.

- An integrated wiki or other knowledge base tool to foster information sharing across the service department.

Security

Although some organizations configure their CRM applications in an "open" manner—where each user can see all information in the application—many need to be able to compartmentalize information. Common examples include sales information, sensitive customer information such as Social Security numbers or account numbers, or even compensation or commission information. A robust security model within your CRM application will give you the flexibility to manage a wide range of different security scenarios.

Key security model functionality to look for includes the following:

- The ability to secure information at both the entity level (for example, accounts, contacts, sales opportunities) and the individual field level (for example, Social Security number)

- The ability to bundle permissions into "roles" that can be assigned to users or groups to facilitate user management

- The ability to handle security exceptions—for when a user needs access to a certain record or set of records outside their current scope of access within the application

- Security that is pervasive throughout the application—applies to viewing information through the user interface, any search or querying tools, and reports and dashboards

Configuration and Customization

CRM applications always require configuration and customization to deliver an elegant user experience and to maximize the value they can provide to your organization. Each organization is different, with different types of customer information to record and different business processes to support with its CRM application. When discussing changes to the CRM application, we use the term *configuration* to describe changes that can be made using the application's administrative tools and features, without programming, and *customization* to describe changing the application via programming. The extent and sophistication of a CRM application's configuration abilities and customization flexibility will determine to what extent you can tailor the application to your present and future needs, as well as the level of effort this tailoring will require.

Key configuration and customization functionality to look for includes the following:

- Ability to extend the application data model without programming. This includes adding new fields to preexisting entities (such as "customer" and "sales opportunity"), as well as designing new entities. These new entities that you define should be fully formed, with the same capabilities as the preexisting entities.

- Ability to insert custom business logic via code into the system to change the way it behaves, typically around system *events* (for example, the creation of a new customer record or the reassignment of a sales opportunity).

- Ability for other applications to interact with the CRM application. Does an application programming interface (API) exist for the application? How robust is it?

Reporting

A large measure of the value of the CRM application is realized through the use of well-designed reports that provide business insight and enable informed decision making. For employees who do not interact with customers, the direct value of the CRM application may be exclusively that gained from CRM reports and dashboards. Don't put too much stock in the out-of-box reports—they are typically too generic to be useful without customization—but rather focus on the report generation tools and the accessibility of the data.

Key reporting functionality to look for includes the following:

- User-focused tools that enable construction of basic reports and dashboards without programming.

- Open access to the data using other reporting tools via standard protocols (for example, ODBC), in a way that respects the application's security model. For example, some applications allow data to be exported to Microsoft Excel for reporting and analysis.

Workflow Automation

If you consider that one of the key functions of your CRM application is to support your customer-facing business processes, the application's workflow automation features are an important focus area.

Without workflow automation, most CRM applications are fundamentally electronic filing cabinets—storing customer information in an organized, searchable way. This is valuable but positions the CRM application as a *passive* participant in any process—a place to retrieve and store information at various steps. It is workflow functionality, combined with custom logic applied to system events, that can make the CRM application an *active* participant in the process. A simple example may be useful to emphasize this difference: consider the case of the handoff of a qualified lead from marketing to the field sales force.

Passive CRM

The marketing rep enters the information from his qualification call onto the lead form. He judges that the lead meets the threshold of "qualified," and he manually reassigns it to the appropriate field sales rep and moves on to the next lead. In the field, sometime in the next few days, the field sales rep logs into CRM and navigates to the list of new leads assigned to her. She opens the lead and reaches out to set up an initial meeting.

Active CRM

The marketing rep enters the information from his qualification call onto the lead form. The CRM application notes that the lead meets the predefined qualification criteria—it automatically changes its status to qualified and reassigns it to the appropriate field sales rep based on the organization's territory sales model. It sends an e-mail to both the marketing rep and the field sales rep to announce the handoff. It starts a timer running; if the field sales rep has not updated the lead in two days, a reminder will be e-mailed to the field sales rep and her manager. In the field, the same day, the field sales rep opens the lead routing e-mail and follows a link in the message to read the marketing reps notes and find contact information for the lead. He reaches out to set up an initial meeting.

The difference should be clear. In the first example, the CRM application is just a repository, where in the second it is an active participant—taking actions and helping foster communications between team members. This type of capability is provided by the CRM application's workflow automation functionality.

Key workflow functionality to look for includes the following:

- The ability to design multistep workflow processes that can respond to application events (for example, creation, update, deletion, reassignment of records) and take a variety of actions (for example, create new records, reassign records, send e-mails or text messages, update records). This should not require programming.

- The ability to branch and control the flow of the workflow process.

- The ability to extend workflow processes with custom logic via code.

Social Media and CRM Applications

Social media tools are emerging as a new communication channel that individuals are using to interact with one another and with organizations. This form of communication is different in significant ways from traditional channels, and organizations need to consider the opportunity it offers for customer engagement. We're defining social media here as tools such as Facebook, Twitter, blogs, wikis, review sites, and video sites that allow individuals to communicate, to create and exchange content, and to find others with similar interests or concerns.

One important aspect of the rise of social media tools is the power they grant individuals to sway public opinion. In the past, an organization needed to manage the opinions of a small set of critical journalists and industry analysts who had the outlets to reach a large audience with whatever message they chose to communicate about the organization. The rise of social media has given every individual the tools to broadly share their dissatisfaction or satisfaction and analysis of an organization. This has significantly complicated the task of the marketing and public relations teams charged with protecting and enhancing an organization's brand.

Social media tools also provide some interesting new capabilities for organizations. Gathering feedback on products and policies is easier and less expensive than with traditional methods (such as focus groups), as is engaging customers in the product planning and design process. Communicating organization updates via Facebook and Twitter reaches individuals in a manner that they are accustomed to and comfortable with.

How can CRM tools help manage an organization's social media presence and communications? Several products exist to provide these capabilities, often integrating with existing mainstream CRM suite applications. The capabilities offered typically include the following:

- Monitoring social media tools (Facebook, Twitter, review sites, blogs, and so on) for references to the organization and helping manage the organization response

- Managing and tracking activity for influential individuals who are widely followed and who publish statements or content about the organization

- Coordinating the organization's proactive communications via social media tools

- Linking an individual's CRM record with their profiles in various social networking sites to provide the CRM users with a fuller picture of the individual and their relationships

Despite the overwhelming popularity of social media, organizations should move carefully and thoughtfully into this channel and consider what customers want to get out of an interaction with them via these tools. Studies have shown that many individuals still perceive social media as tools to connect with friends and family members and may not welcome an aggressive presence by organizations.

Expectations

It isn't easy. Both the initial launch of a CRM program and its ongoing stewardship require significant time and energy from a spectrum of individuals within your organization. At the same time that you are increasing your expectations around the effort involved, it's equally important to restrain your expectations about outcomes, especially as you launch your program. CRM can be a big change for organizations, and change can be slow and yield modest early benefits.

As outlined in detail in Chapters 5 and 6, successfully launching a CRM program and then maintaining and growing it are significant undertakings. The initial project will represent a significant investment of capital and of time and energy from a set of individuals across your business, technology, and executive teams. These individuals will need to come together, collaborate, and make decisions swiftly to support the CRM launch. They will need to work as tireless cheerleaders and role models to help the CRM seed take root and grow into a source of significant and lasting value for the organization. The ongoing maintenance and enhancement of CRM requires that the steering committee and CRM administration team faithfully execute a set of processes to regularly identify, prioritize, and execute minor needs and improvements, as well as to plan larger initiatives to align the CRM program with the goals of the organization and to expand its reach and value.

If we make the process of launching and managing a CRM program sound like a siege, this is only to make a small contribution toward reigning in the rampant marketing of the CRM vendors, who consistently send the dangerous message that if only you will purchase their application and install it, all will be right with your organization, and you will begin to reap the benefit of a business that is in tune with itself and its customers. CRM applications *can* have an amazing positive impact on your business, and they *can* help you transform into a nimble organization that delivers outstanding customer experiences and can turn on a dime to capitalize on new opportunities. But the application can't do it for you—you have to "own" your CRM program and understand that you are responsible for its success. This is why we consider "reasonable expectations" a critical component of a successful CRM program—reasonable expectations around the effort required, the costs, the short-term outcomes, and the longer-term ones.

Setting Expectations for Customer-Facing Employees

Your customer-facing employees are likely to have both their processes and the tools that they use changed as part of the launch of a CRM program. This will not be accomplished without some pain and some friction—as the libraries of books on change management can attest. The ultimate success of the CRM program will depend on this group embracing it and overcoming any transition difficulties. To help ensure this outcome, the following points need to be communicated to this group:

- The overall vision for the CRM program, its intended benefits, and the linkage between the program and the organization's strategic goals should be communicated to help secure employee buy-in.

- The CRM steering committee understands that there will be hiccups and issues as the program is launched—employees' patience is appreciated, their feedback is desired, and budget has been set aside to clear obstacles and address their concerns.

- Despite any transition challenges, management's commitment to the CRM program will not waver. This is not a "trial" or a "test" or an "experiment" but rather a key organization strategy and how "business is done" from now on. We need to all get it right together.

Pitfalls

Now that we have reviewed the people, process, technology, and expectations needed to assemble a successful CRM program, it is likely instructive to highlight a few ways we have seen organizations either fail or unwittingly introduce obstacles to their CRM success. Take care to avoid repeating these mistakes with your own CRM program.

Poor Executive Sponsorship

As discussed in the prior section, launching a CRM program can be a lot of work for the implementation team and for all impacted employees in the weeks after launch. Things will not be perfect out of the gate, and there may be a frustrating period of refining the processes and application and ramping up. Some employees may be tempted to revert to old ways of doing things and may resist using the CRM application. If these employees are high performers, for example, top salespeople, managers may be tempted to look the other way. This is corrosive—sending the message to others that CRM is "optional," and diminishing the value of the program by putting some customer information and interactions outside the CRM processes and CRM application.

The CRM executive sponsor must be prepared to tackle adoption challenges of this type. The sponsor must continually sell the vision of CRM throughout the organization, emphasize its value, and hold everyone accountable to fully participate in the CRM program. At the same time, this person must work to keep the CRM program nimble and to incorporate employee feedback to eliminate issues and drive improvements into the program so that all employees benefit.

Not Engaging "Doers" As Stakeholders

We have been involved in many CRM projects where it has become apparent that management is disconnected from how work actually gets done by customer-facing employees. We have been in meetings where a manager is describing how a process works and an individual sales representative has contradicted them, saying "But that isn't really how it happens."

Engaging customer-facing employees in the design and development of the CRM program is needed for many reasons:

- As in the previous example, sometimes only the customer-facing employees—the salespeople and customer service staff—know how processes actually work and how tools are actually used. The foundation of any kind of process improvement or CRM application design is a clear understanding of how things work today.

- CRM processes will be executed and CRM applications will be used by these employees, so it is only logical that they have a voice in how they are designed. They offer a unique, valuable perspective that managers and executives cannot provide.

- They provide a usability "check" during the design of the CRM application. A business analyst may want 50 different data attributes to be captured about a customer to allow the analyst to segment and analyze the customer base. A representative of the sales employees can push back based on usability concerns, knowing what is truly feasible based on who the salespeople are speaking with and what information is available to them.

- Ultimately, the success of the CRM program will hinge on the adoption of the CRM processes and applications by the customer-facing team. If these employees feel as though their voices were heard during the design and that these are "their processes" and "their application," rather than something foisted on them by IT or senior management, they will have more buy-in and will be stronger supporters of the program. They will also be more vocal in providing positive feedback to help improve it.

Implementing a CRM Program Without a Clear Roadmap

"Measure twice, cut once." What is true for carpentry is true for CRM programs. Preparation and careful planning will yield a more successful CRM program with greater employee satisfaction. We will cover roadmap planning and development in detail in Chapter 3, but fundamentally it is about thinking critically and strategically about the CRM initiatives that will provide the most benefit to the organization, considering other factors such as synergies between different initiatives, and laying out and communicating a phased plan.

Proceeding without a roadmap has the potential to be inefficient (not necessarily addressing the highest value areas first), confusing (people can't look forward to understand what is happening when and why), and expensive (often areas need to be reworked and redesigned as they are impacted by subsequent initiatives). In addition, the fits and starts that accompany implementing CRM without a solid plan sap momentum from the program and undercut the credibility of the team.

Providing Inadequate Training

Training is an area that, for whatever reason, executives tend to focus on when trying to reduce the costs of a proposed CRM project. "Our people are smart" or "This is not rocket science" are comments that often precede slashing budgets for training. For project managers planning a CRM initiative, the training effort is often addressed as an afterthought and does not get the same level of planning, preparation, and focus as the other project components.

In fact, effective training is a key driver of user adoption and overall program success. Training should be role-tailored and scenario-based and should blend process and application training so that employees learn how the process works and how to use the CRM application to support it. A hands-on component is valuable to keeping trainees engaged. In addition to initial prelaunch training, it is wise to plan for follow-on training and informal question-and-answer sessions to help the CRM team monitor the success of the employees in adopting the CRM processes and tools and to provide employees with many opportunities to get their questions answered.

Skipping Data Migration or Data Cleanup

Programmatically migrating clean data into a new CRM application prior to launch adds value in a number of ways. It reduces data entry work for employees; it reduces or eliminates the occasions where users need to go back to their old tools, helping to cement the switch to the CRM application; and it allows for meaningful reports that compare post-CRM data with pre-CRM data to be run more easily from within the CRM application.

However, data migration is an area of considerable effort, expense, and complexity in most CRM initiatives and is therefore often an attractive target for budget cutting. Executives should consider eliminating this work only after a thoughtful and realistic assessment of the impact on the CRM users to make sure they are balancing cost saving with program risk appropriately.

Not Providing Value to All Stakeholders

The CRM program will naturally provide value in different ways to the different stakeholder groups. Managers and executives will look to CRM reports and analytics to gain insight into their business and customers to help them make better decisions and better predict future performance. Customer-facing employees should find that the CRM application helps them stay organized and be more productive and helps minimize the administrative overhead associated with their job function.

It's possible to craft an initial CRM project that focuses on delivering value for one group and fails to deliver value for another. This is a hazardous approach and one to be avoided at all costs. Careful attention should be paid during the planning for your CRM roadmap to make sure each group engaged in a project is getting at least some value from it.

To illustrate this risk, consider a basic initial CRM program launch that involves deploying a new sales methodology for a group of salespeople and a new CRM application for them to use to manage their sales activities.

Extreme, Flawed Approach #1

Imagine a project team that, fearful of user adoption problems, focuses on making the use of the sales methodology and CRM application as painless as possible for the sales representatives. Every time they complain that the application makes them enter too much information about their activity, the team adjusts by removing details and simplifying. Steps that the reps are uncomfortable with are diluted or removed from the methodology. At the end of the day, the result is a watered-down methodology of unknown effectiveness and an application that the users grumblingly support but that does not gather enough information to do any analysis or even to create a complete pipeline.

The lack of value for management causes them to revert to their old ad hoc approaches of managing the sales team. Their lack of interest in the tool becomes clear to the salespeople, who slowly disengage until no one uses it any longer.

Extreme, Flawed Approach #2

The project team in this example spends most of its time with the executive team, understanding what kinds of sales dashboards and analytics they would like to see and how they would like to be able to segment sales information. To support these rich reporting requirements, the resulting methodology and CRM application are highly structured—requiring sales representatives to enter every minute action they take as part of the sales cycle and to enter vast amounts of information about their opportunities, contacts, and prospects. Little attention is paid to the sales representatives' "day in the life" or to what kind of process and application functionality would help them be more effective. Sales reps objections are countered with "This is what the executives need—this project has their full support."

The result is a bloated, onerous process and CRM application that sales representatives dread. No two reps use the tool the same way—its complexity leaves many options for how to use it. Eventually it slows reps down so much that they start ignoring it until the end of the month, when they know managers run their forecast reports. Then in one frantic push, they enter in the minimum required information for all their activity for the month. Salespeople are unhappy—the process and application are a "tax" on their work and do not help them at all. Managers complain that the reports are right only once a month and the salespeople won't use the application.

These examples are purposefully extreme to illustrate the point that you need to try to craft the project so that there is a win for each stakeholder group and each group is more productive than before.

Trying to Do Too Much at Once

We have seen clients attempt to roll their entire roadmap into a single project—this "big-bang" approach seeks to launch the CRM program for all planned departments and all business functions in one shot. Although this approach appears to have the advantage of achieving all the organization's CRM goals in the shortest possible time, it is high-risk and has a number of disadvantages when compared to a multiproject, roadmap approach. Most of these projects collapse under their own weight—there are too many stakeholders with conflicting priorities, there are too many interconnections that paralyze every decision, and the project duration is too long, resulting in team member and sponsor burnout and turnover.

The multiple-project approach, by contrast, offers a number of key advantages:

- Shorter, sequential projects translate to less time before the organization starts to see value from CRM, helping to build momentum behind the program.

- Getting some processes and departments live while working on others allows for lessons learned to be fed into future projects, increasing the overall program quality.

- Small, focused projects are easier to execute successfully—there are few people and fewer "moving parts," and the project objectives are fewer and can be more closely aligned.

Summary

The components of a successful CRM program fall into three categories: people, processes, and technology.

- In the people category, there are a host of important roles. Most important are the executive sponsor, who acts as the leader of the program and must set the direction and keep everyone else moving forward, and the departmental champions, who keep their teams engaged and channel their feedback to the CRM administration team.

- Process has a dual meaning in the context of CRM; there are a host of business processes that can be enhanced and supported with the CRM application, and then there are a set of operational processes that must be put into place to manage the CRM program. Designing these operational processes is an important step in preparing to launch a CRM program.

- In addition to the CRM application, technology components include a source control application and a plan for maintaining test and development environments for the CRM application.

CHAPTER 3

Building a CRM Roadmap

Establishing a well-considered, thoughtful plan for implementing a CRM program can help you strike the best balance between your organization's priorities and initiatives and the needs and preparedness of different departments. A haphazard, unplanned implementation can result in disjointed business processes, dissatisfied employees, and excessive implementation costs. When it comes to planning your CRM program, "An ounce of prevention is worth a pound of cure."

In this chapter, we'll review the process of outlining a one- to three-year plan for your CRM program, which we'll refer to as your *roadmap*. All organizations should develop and maintain a CRM roadmap—whether they are just beginning to think about CRM or whether they have a successful, mature program in place. The roadmap is a constantly evolving document, reflecting your changing business situation and priorities and maintaining that one- to three-year look into the future. In the next section, we will consider the rationale behind a phased approach to CRM. Then we will explore the development of your initial roadmap.

Why a Phased Approach to Your CRM Program?

When you have developed your initial vision for your overall CRM program, it may be tempting to try to realize the entire scope with a single project. This appears to be the most direct and shortest path to achieving the vision. We strongly discourage this type of "big-bang" approach, where your organization attempts to move from "no CRM" to "full CRM vision" in a single project. In this section, we hope to convince you that a phased approach, whereby several smaller projects are chained together to progress toward the complete vision and grow the footprint of CRM, is a much more sensible approach and will increase the success of your program. Building internal momentum for one big push may seem easier, and rolling out the program to all employees at once seems simpler than coordinating multiple phases, but do not be fooled.

The following sections are a few of the problems with the "big bang" that are addressed via a phased approach.

It Takes Too Long

The longer the duration of a business process and technology application project like CRM, the greater the likelihood of failure, because of a number of factors. Turnover on the project team saps the team of its institutional memory—decisions are rehashed and redebated as new team members join, further slowing project progress. The larger the project scope, the more stakeholders must be involved, demanding a voice in the decision making and resulting in a slower, committee-driven project. Fatigue saps the energy from the project sponsor and other executives, who grow weary of selling the benefits of a project to increasingly skeptical employees who grow to doubt that the program will ever launch. The longer the project duration, the more time elapses between the design of the CRM processes and application and their rollout. At the pace of business change today, the longer this time period, the further out of alignment the program will be with the reality on the ground and the needs of the employees when it actually launches.

In a phased approach, each project is smaller in scope and shorter in duration, with fewer objectives and stakeholders. Each project builds on the prior and expands the reach of CRM within your organization, addressing a new department or business process. We will introduce guidelines for how to break your program into phases to build your roadmap later in this chapter.

There Are No Opportunities to Incorporate Feedback

With a phased approach, there is the opportunity to do a post-project review after each project phase and incorporate lessons learned and successful practices into the next phase so that your project execution is theoretically improving with each phase as you refine your project methodology to best suit your organization. With the big bang, there are fewer opportunities for this type of learning, because each stage in the project is fundamentally executed a single time.

Building Your Initial Roadmap

In this section, we'll focus on the process to build your initial roadmap to launch your CRM program. If you have already established a CRM program and deployed a CRM application, we'll cover the special case of developing a roadmap after you've already implemented a CRM application in the "Developing a Roadmap Midstream" section.

Assess Your Current Situation

The heart of roadmap planning is assessing your current situation and your strategic goals; a study of these should suggest a set of initiatives that then need to be ordered and scheduled appropriately to maximize efficiency and minimize risk.

Current Business Processes

A useful first step in building your roadmap is to document your current business processes as they function today. You may find inconsistencies in process across employees or departments that perform similar functions—this is common. Many of your planned CRM initiatives may require process changes, and having the current state documented will help map out and create understanding of the implications of changes. This work may also reveal inefficiencies, processes that create a poor customer experience, or opportunities to share best practices from one user or department to another. In general, you should strive for process consistency whenever it is practical—there are a host of benefits from all employees and departments tackling the same task in the same way, and to the extent this consistency is felt by the customer, it will improve his or her experience as well.

Current Customer Information Applications

Create a catalog of the different applications used to manage customer information or customer-related processes. This catalog should describe who uses each application, for what purpose, and how the application is used in the context of your organization's processes. Interview users to understand their perception of each application's strengths and limitations. This process is likely to be eye-opening. Most organizations develop their processes and tools in grassroots, bottom-up fashion, in reaction to changing circumstances, and with little strategic perspective. You will likely find multiple applications that hold the same information, processes that require redundant entry into multiple applications, and an abundance of small, Microsoft Excel or Access solutions to solve specific problems. This tapestry of applications can hinder user productivity and prevent effective collaboration between your employees. We are not suggesting that there should be a single, monolithic application within an organization but simply that your array of applications should be the result of a rational plan—selected to maximize employee productivity and effectiveness and provide a superior customer experience. In most organizations, this is not the case.

Find the Pain

Part of your assessment process is to "find the pain" in your customer-facing teams. At the risk of stating the obvious, these pain points may signal a people/process/technology breakdown that needs to be addressed. So, follow the complaints. Who is arguing for change? What team or function consistently fails to meet expectations? Is there more employee turnover? Analyze the situation—what is causing the underlying problem? Who is impacted, and what is the business value of addressing the pain? Is addressing this pain in line with the organization's strategic goals?

Strategic Goals

Your organization's strategic goals and strategic plan play an important role in shaping your CRM roadmap. They may be a direct source of initiatives for the roadmap. For example, if your plan includes entering a new market or pursuing a new customer segment, this will likely require CRM people, process, and technology changes to support the effort. In addition to directly contributing to your set of CRM initiatives, your strategic goals also serve as an important lens on evaluating initiatives for inclusion in the CRM roadmap. For example, you might deprioritize initiatives to support a product line or sales channel that is becoming less relevant or being phased out because of a new strategic direction.

Technology Issues

Most CRM programs involve a technology component, so it is helpful as part of your assessment to understand your technology landscape and what the IT roadmap looks like within your organization so that you can align your own roadmap accordingly. For example, if your IT organization is planning a complete overhaul of your corporate web platform in Q3, you probably should not invest in integrating your CRM application and your web site in Q2. Major application deployments, IT head count changes, and IT skill set changes can all impact your roadmap and should be understood and factored into your planning.

Red Flags

Early detection of "red flags"—issues that may endanger the success of your program—gives you the most time to formulate a plan to neutralize or avoid them. As you conduct your assessment, keep a running list of red flags you identify, and consider how to address them. Common red flags that we have seen in pursuing CRM programs successfully include the following:

- *Weak executive sponsorship or buy-in*: For example, a sales leader who does not understand or believe in the value of CRM will make a successful sales-focused program very difficult. Significant turnover at the executive level can also make development of the CRM program difficult, because each new leader wants to impose his or her own priorities on the program, and CRM does not get a chance to build momentum in any one direction.

- *Limited IT resources, combined with an unwillingness to invest in consulting assistance*: To continually improve and adjust to changing business circumstances, your CRM application will require regular investment. Organizations without IT resources (for example, developers, testers) need to be ready to contract for these skills to ensure the vitality of their program. An area where we often see insufficient investment is in reporting, where organizations seem to chronically underestimate the effort involved. This is a red flag because effective reporting and analytics are a critical source of CRM value for management.

- *Weak business analysis skills within affected departments*: CRM programs need a detailed-oriented, dedicated management team to make them successful. These teams need individuals who understand the organization and its processes and have enough application savvy to help translate the business needs into application capabilities.

Split Your CRM Vision into Projects

Once you have completed your assessment, you should have a number of departments and business processes identified that could be improved, with respect to either their people (for example, how they are staffed, what employee roles and responsibilities are, and so on), their processes, or their technology tools. The next goal is to assemble these into discrete projects and sequence those projects against a calendar. This is the heart of the roadmap development. We described earlier in this chapter the rationale behind a phased implementation approach and will not revisit that here; in this section we want to provide some perspectives that you should consider to understand how to group your various needs into individual projects and how to sequence them in the most advantageous way. There are no hard-and-fast rules, but there are a set of considerations that will be helpful:

- *Business impact*: You will learn from your assessment what areas of your organization have the greatest need and where there is the greatest potential for increased productivity and effectiveness. Barring all other factors, it makes sense to pursue these areas first.

- *By department*: Centering a project around a single department can have a number of advantages; it minimizes the number of stakeholders involved, making project management easier. The more of their work an individual employee can complete with just a single tool (the CRM application), the more likely they are to see the value in the tool and adopt it.

- *By business process*: It can be disjointed and unworkable to change only *part* of a business process. Imagine, for example, a software organization with a customer service organization and a software quality team. Issues are often escalated from customer service to software quality, when the issue is related to a software defect. Imagine transitioning the customer service issue management process to your new CRM application but leaving the old Access database in place for the software quality team. Issues would be smoothly escalated through customer service, with CRM workflow handling reassignments and notifications. Then, when escalation is needed to software quality, the process just "falls off a cliff"— customer service reps end up cutting and pasting information from the CRM service case into an e-mail to someone on the software quality team. If and when that person gets to it, they must cut and paste the details from the e-mail into the Access system to be worked by their team. There is no automation or workflow from this point. Customer service has no visibility from their CRM application into the status of the issue once it is in software quality, so they cannot give customers any information when they call but rather must take a message and follow up. This is not ideal for your employees and not ideal for your customers and is the result of spreading the same business process across multiple CRM projects.

- *By geography*: Organizations with geographically dispersed teams that each work with their own local customers are potential candidates for separate CRM projects. Remote and/or smaller teams that tend to handle multiple processes in a location are often receptive and eager to be part of a pilot program that streamlines their process.

- *By duration/effort*: Large CRM projects can bog down and in some cases collapse under their own weight—caught in endless cycles of analysis or never-ending development phases. All else being equal, there is value in having the first one or two projects in your roadmap be fairly small in scope and low in risk. If you can get some set of employees up and running with the program and start seeing some benefits for the organization, it will help build momentum behind CRM in your organization and will dispel fears that CRM is "not real" or "will never happen." You'll also begin to get real feedback from employees that you can feed into future projects to improve them.

Another factor to consider in designing projects is outcomes—how will success or failure be judged for each project? What are the outcomes that each department expects from the projects that involve it? Ideally each project would include clear, agreed-upon success factors so that there is an objective way to gauge a project's outcome.

Line Up the People

Once your CRM assessment is complete and you have developed a preliminary roadmap of projects based on the factors outlined in the prior section, your roadmap planning work is not yet complete. The effort required to launch a CRM program is significant, and it is therefore important to evaluate your draft roadmap from the "people perspective." Plan an individual conversation with the leaders of each department impacted by your roadmap to explore the following:

- *Bandwidth*: Does the department have a clear understanding of the "asks" that will be made of them by the CRM team for the CRM projects that involve their department? Can the department free the right people for the necessary time to make the project successful? Your CRM team cannot deliver successful CRM projects on their own—each project should be viewed as a partnership between the CRM team and the departments involved. You need to confirm that each department is ready and able to pull their own weight and participate fully.

- *Buy-in*: Different executives within your organization will have different levels of "belief" in the CRM program and its benefits. You may find that some are skeptical or even hostile, based on poor experiences in their past or on the nature of their team. They may view the CRM program as a "distraction." As we have discussed previously, strong, evangelical executive support is a key success factor for CRM projects, so if you encounter these types of attitudes, consider it a significant red flag. You probably want to be thoughtful about how to schedule and structure projects with departments led by "CRM skeptics." For example, avoid addressing these departments with your initial project; it's better to get some early wins with other groups and build momentum behind CRM before tackling these departments. If you must include them early in your roadmap, attempt to broaden the project to include departments led by strong "CRM believer" executives of similar rank to help ensure strong executive leadership.

Pilots and the "Proof-of-Concept" Project

Pilots and "proof-of-concept" projects can be considered just another type of CRM project that should be fit into your roadmap as needed. These special projects serve a specific purpose—to validate a specific element (that is, process or technology tool) in a small-scale, low-risk way prior to a larger-scale project. The two terms are often used interchangeably, but in our lexicon they have distinct meanings.

A *pilot* refers to a complete project that delivers the changes planned for the entire organization to a small segment to get a preview of what the results will be for the entire organization. The project is complete in that the affected segment changes the way they conduct actual business; it is not a simulation or test. For example, before rolling out a new process and technology tool for collaborative customer proposal generation to 2,000 U.S.-based field sales personnel, an organization might choose instead to pilot it by rolling it out to the 100 salespeople in the Los Angeles office for a period of six months. This approach minimizes the organization's risk—if the changes have a negative impact or otherwise fail to deliver on their goals, only 5 percent of the sales organization is affected. The downside is of course the delay; if it proves wildly successful, the organization has lost six months of benefit to the rest of the sales team via the pilot approach. Critical to a successful pilot is an up-front consideration of outcomes—what outcome will trigger an organization-wide rollout, and what will trigger rework or abandonment of the effort? How will these outcomes be measured, and by whom?

A *proof-of-concept* is a more limited project, generally intended to prove a technology tool before full development. In a proof-of-concept, no change is made to how the organization conducts its actual business; it is simply a research project to explore whether something can be done in some small way before attempting to do it in a large way. For example, imagine that a paper products company wants to outfit its field sales team with a mobile device that will allow them to initiate a variety of transactions in the company's ERP application (for example, placing a new order, checking an order status, getting approval for a discount) from a customer's location. The mobile device vendor assures the company that this can be done, but they have no experience integrating their device to the company's ERP application, and they have a limited understanding of the company's network security that would need to be navigated to allow remote transactions. Before embarking on a full design and development project to roll the device out to the global sales force, the company elects to conduct a proof-of-concept. The goal is to build a light sample application that can connect to the company's ERP application from a remote location and retrieve an order status. This is a dramatically smaller project with limited design and development work (the application does not need to look good or be easy to use—no salespeople will ever see it, and it needs to support only a single type of transaction). But if successful, it *proves* that the vendor can navigate the company's network security and interact with the ERP application. Proving these points eliminates much of the risk associated with the larger project. As with the pilot example, the trade-off for this risk mitigation is time and dollars—the full project is on hold while the proof-of-concept is delivered, and including a proof-of-concept project increases the overall cost of the initiative. As with the pilot, thoughtful consideration of what the goals of the poof-of-concept are, and what outcome constitutes "proof," should precede the project.

Both pilots and proof-of-concept projects can be useful to control risk in your CRM program, but they have a schedule and cost impact that must be considered.

A Sample Roadmap Exercise

In this example, we'll consider the case of IdeaShare, a fictional maker of payment-processing software. IdeaShare has been on a slow but steady growth path over the past few years but has recently undergone a leadership change. The new leadership wants to pursue growth more aggressively with the goal of either a public offering or an acquisition. To drive this growth, they have developed a new strategic plan that includes goals to increase IdeaShare's business in the education and government markets where they are currently not active, invest in customer service to eliminate a reputation for poor service that is suspected to be interfering with sales, develop a partner sales channel, and accelerate the development of IdeaShare's next-generation product. Fiona Smith, the IdeaShare COO, has been tasked by the CEO and owners with exploring a CRM program at IdeaShare.

Please note that the goal of this example is to help illuminate the concepts from this chapter; we've prioritized this goal over attempts to make the example too realistic.

CRM Assessment Results

Fiona began work on the CRM program with a month of interviews. She spoke to individuals at various levels in IdeaShare's sales, marketing, customer service, product development, and information technology groups. She interviewed customers and prospective customers about their experience with IdeaShare. Sifting through her notes, Fiona observed the following:

Sales

- Most sales processes were either e-mail or Microsoft Excel driven. Forecasting was fairly primitive, based on Excel. Each year, the lowest-performing 10 percent of reps were replaced. There was little collaboration or professional development activity.

- There was no domain experience in government or education markets in the sales organization.

- The new sales vice president, who had been in the role only one month, had experience with CRM applications and was desperate for the chance to bring one into the organization.

Marketing

- Marketing consisted of a presence at three key annual tradeshows for IdeaShare's industry, print advertising in key trade journals, web advertising, and mass e-mail marketing.

- The marketing team used a sophisticated Microsoft Access database, developed by the marketing director, to manage their activity. The marketing director was dismissive of CRM, indicating that he had "used them all," and that none was as tailored to their business as his database.

- The primary complaint from marketing was lack of feedback from sales on their leads—no one ever bothered to "close the loop" and let them know what happened with leads.

- Marketing was largely perceived within the company as a well-run, effective group.

Customer Service

- Issues were reported via phone or e-mail by customers. E-mail issues were forwarded from support@ideashare.com to the entire team of 15 customer service representatives, who used e-mail to "claim" issues to work on. There was no visibility to issues being worked on by individual representatives. The customer service manager monitored e-mail to prevent any issues from "slipping through the cracks."

- Customer service reps had to bounce between three applications to serve customers—the billing application to handle billing issues, the licensing application to handle license problems, and the bug tracker to view the status of issues escalated to the product development team.

- The customer service manager's sense of their department's process was anecdotal; developing any metrics was a laborious process.

- The time to ramp up a new service rep was long; most knowledge of common issues and solution was "tribal," held in the minds of the senior service reps. During their "apprenticeship," new reps could rarely address issues on the first call and often had to engage the senior reps.

Information Technology

- The information technology team is kept lean. Its staff can maintain the company's network and key applications and provide help-desk support to users but does not have budget or head count for new initiatives. Team members are by and large pure "technicians" rather than businesspeople who understand technology.

Customers and Prospective Customers

- Customers were generally satisfied with IdeaShare's products but routinely unhappy with the service they receive. Complaints included long times to resolve issues and ill-informed service reps who seemed to provide different answers to the same issues depending on the day of the week.

- Large or small, customers praised the sales team's understanding of their needs and willingness to invest time to help them understand IdeaShare's products and which ones would best meet their needs.

Preliminary Roadmap

Fiona's reviewed her notes and observations and came to the following conclusions about each group's potential for the CRM program.

Sales

The sales team needed more structure in how they approached and managed the sales activity. "Primitive" forecasting would not cut it for an organization that hoped to go public or court a suitor for an acquisition. A defined and consistent sales process, combined with a modern CRM application, could solve the forecasting problem. The planned partner channel would also necessitate a more robust application than Excel to track partner sales activity. From a personnel standpoint, the lack of education and government sector background was troubling, given the strategic goal around these markets. Fiona concluded that an overlay sales team, composed of outside hires with the needed domain background, would be needed to succeed in these markets. Lastly, the fact that small and large customers alike reported getting "lots of time" from the IdeaShare sales team was a cause for concern for Fiona. Were reps making smart decisions about where to invest their selling time? Did they have the information they needed to judge the potential of their prospects? This seemed like another potential area for improvement via the CRM program.

Marketing

Fiona knew that a combination of process modification on the sales side, asking reps to catalog the outcome of a lead before closing it out, and a shared CRM application between marketing and sales could solve marketing's lead visibility problem. She also knew that marketing's Access database would not cut it when the group was asked to ramp up lead generation and distribute generated leads to the new partner channel. So, there was clearly a role for CRM here. However, the company partner channel plans were later in the strategic plan, and the marketing director clearly needed some convincing to support the CRM program. She concluded that marketing should not be the initial focus of the CRM program.

Customer Service

The lack of a structured issue management process and an application to support it was the fundamental problem here, Fiona concluded. Not only would this prevent issues from slipping through the cracks, but the increased understanding of the types of issues most commonly faced could inform new rep training and shorten their ramp-up. Managing issues via the CRM application rather than in e-mail would also allow for easier generation of metrics to monitor the group's operations. A knowledge base tool, which would provide to reps a searchable place to pool their knowledge, procedures, and best practices, was also an important need; it would help new reps ramp up and free some of the coaching burden from senior reps. Lastly, Fiona predicted that some thoughtful CRM integration could minimize the number of different applications reps needed to juggle to handle issues.

Information Technology

The lean nature of the IT team was a red flag for Fiona. Success in the CRM program would require a person on the technology side with a solid business understanding and the ability to translate business needs into technology requirements and to manage the technical effort associated with CRM. They also had to be able to dedicate 75 to 100 percent of their time to the CRM program. Fiona then laid out a preliminary roadmap for the CRM program, as shown in Table 3-1.

Table 3-1. *Preliminary Roadmap for the CRM Program*

Project Element	Groups Impacted	Notes
YEAR 1 :: QUARTER 1		
Standardize and document issue management process.	Customer service	
Design and deploy CRM application to support issue management.	Customer service	
Design and deploy customer service dashboard based on CRM.	Customer service	
Hire CRM analyst.	Information technology	
YEAR 1 :: QUARTER 2		
Standardize and document sales process.	Sales	
Onboard sales team to CRM application for opportunity and	Sales	Retire Excel-based forecast tool.

Project Element	Groups Impacted	Notes
forecast management.		
Design and deploy sales dashboard and forecast report.	Sales	
Create guidelines for contributing to new customer service knowledge base. Launch incentive program to drive authorship and adoption.	Customer service	
Deploy knowledge base features of CRM application.	Customer service	
YEAR 1 :: QUARTER 3		
Document overlay sales team organization, sales process, compensation plan.	Sales	
Update CRM application to reflect overlay sales team processes.	Sales	
Hire government and education sales team.	Sales	
YEAR 1 :: QUARTER 4		
Move lead tracking and assignment process into CRM application.	Marketing	Retire Access for lead tracking and assignment.
Design and deploy lead dashboard for marketing that shows outcome of all leads handed off to sales.	Marketing	
Hire CRM developer.	Information technology	
YEAR 2 :: QUARTER 1		
Implement application integration project to eliminate	Customer service	

Project Element	Groups Impacted	Notes
reps having to juggle apps.		
Move e-mail marketing, advertising, and trade show management into CRM.	Marketing	Retire Access completely.
Assess performance of the government and education sales team.	Sales	Six-month review of the new sales team. Is it meeting its goals? What is working, and what is not? CRM can provide metrics to inform the process.
YEAR 2 :: QUARTER 2		
Pilot mobile client for CRM.	Sales	
Develop lead scoring feature in CRM to help salespeople prioritize their sales time.	Sales	
Deploy web portal so that customers can create and update service issues via the Web.	Customer service	

Fiona's next step is to meet with her leadership team, as well as individually with the leaders of sales, marketing, customer service, and information technology departments to refine the roadmap and to discuss outcomes/success factors (for example, what does "complete" mean for each of these items?).

Developing a Roadmap Midstream

The sample roadmap in the previous section describes a scenario where an organization, IdeaShare, is planning its initial launch of a CRM program. But what if your organization has already rolled out a CRM program and application and your goal is to apply more rigor to the management of the program to help more employees get more value from CRM? The general two-step process outlined in this chapter, assessment followed by roadmap planning, still applies to this situation. In some ways, this situation is easier than starting "from scratch." Employees are already familiar with the concepts of CRM and with your organization's chosen CRM application. The challenge is that "you never get a second chance to make a first impression." Employees have an opinion about CRM that may be difficult to change and, if negative, may hamper future CRM initiatives. In this situation, it is even more important to make sure the roadmap development process is transparent and inclusive.

Summary

This chapter covered the following:

- A phased approach to implementing CRM, consisting of multiple smaller projects, is a more effective, lower-risk approach than attempting a single large project.

- Begin your roadmap planning with a detailed assessment of your current situation.

- Lining up the people is a critical part of roadmap planning to ensure that the impacted groups have the bandwidth and motivation to support CRM.

- Consider both pilot and proof-of-concept projects if appropriate for your situation.

CHAPTER 4

Evaluating Software and Consultants

In the previous two chapters, we saw that a successful CRM program is a combination of people, business process, and technology that come together to help an organization achieve its CRM goals. Although the technology supporting CRM programs is only one component, it can have a significant impact on the success of the program. Many organizations have seen their CRM programs hindered or even abandoned because of expensive, inflexible, or difficult-to-use CRM applications.

The goal of this chapter is to provide a process and a set of key criteria that you can use to select both the appropriate CRM application and the right consulting partner to support your CRM program. While we describe the evaluation of software and consultants separately, in practice the processes are often intertwined, because CRM vendors typically engage partners early in the sales cycle. A CRM application may be the clear "winner" in your software evaluation, but if it is poorly supported from a consulting perspective, you may want to make a different selection.

The CRM Software Market

The CRM software market is broad and rapidly changing. Rather than including a detailed catalog of the current leading applications, in this section we will describe some of the key variables across CRM products to help you understand how to compare and categorize applications. These variables include the functional scope, deployment options, application access, and licensing model.

Functional Scope: Full CRM Suites and Specialty Applications

The traditional CRM "suite" includes features to support three front-office business functions: marketing, sales, and customer service. Sales functionality typically includes lead and sales opportunity management and quote development. Marketing functionality allows for segregating leads and customers and coordinating communication with those leads across a variety of mediums (e-mail, telephone, and direct mail). Customer service is typically comprised of issue management and a knowledge base. The promised value of the full CRM suite, aside from the value derived within each department from the application's features, is the information sharing that it can foster *across* departments. Such sharing is necessary if the organization is going to present a single face to the customer.

There are also a host of more specialized CRM applications that target specific business functions (for example, marketing demand generation, customer service and support), specific environments (applications for call centers), or specific industries (wealth management, nonprofits). These may be less expensive or more feature-rich in their area than the full suite products, but careful consideration should be given prior to selecting a specialty application. The challenge of integrating several specialized, departmental applications together to get a seamless customer view may outweigh any advantages these applications may have over a CRM suite.

Deployment Models

There are several options for deploying CRM applications within your organization, with varying costs, risks, and benefits. In this section we will review the most common three: on-premises, application hosting/colocation, and software-as-a-service.

On-Premises

This is the traditional model of deploying client-server software application such as CRM applications; the customer installs the software on their own server hardware at their own premises. This deployment model gives the customer maximum control, because they can select and upgrade the server hardware as needed. They can implement whatever backup and disaster recovery plan they prefer. This scenario also facilitates integration scenarios; authentication and network security complications are typically fewer than if the CRM application was hosted outside the company network. The drawback of this model is its costs, in terms of server hardware and IT personnel.

At the lower end of the CRM market are applications that are "client only," rather than "client-server." These applications are intended as individual productivity tools, typically for salespeople. The veteran application in this space is ACT! Others include GoldMine and Business Contact Manager from Microsoft. These applications can be great personal productivity tools but are not suitable for organizations seeking to foster information sharing and collaboration as part of their CRM programs. Although many of these vendors have introduced multiuser, networked versions of their products to try to compete at the low end of the CRM market, in our experience this is a case where "the leopard can't change its spots." These products are fundamentally not designed for organization-wide use and should be avoided.

Application Hosting and Server Colocation

In this model, the customer purchases the software and then installs and uses it from server hardware at a third party's location. The customer may own the servers (colocation) or not (application hosting). The software licenses may be licensed on a perpetual or subscription basis. In the case of application hosting, the provider typically provides server maintenance, backup, and disaster recovery. In the colocation model, the provider may only supply power and network connectivity. These deployment models offer a lighter IT burden than on-premises, with less control.

Software-as-a-Service

The software-as-a-service (SaaS) model, pioneered in the CRM market by Salesforce.com, has established itself and is gaining momentum, buoyed by the recent rise of cloud computing as an accepted alternative to managing one's own technology infrastructure. This model seeks to transform enterprise software from a capital asset to a utility service that is purchased and consumed.

Perhaps the simplest way to understand software-as-a-service is as a combination of subscription licensing (as described earlier) and outsourced, off-site server infrastructure. In its most common form, customers are charged on a per-user/per-month basis and pay via credit card. The software is accessed via the Internet, and the customer has no visibility, responsibility, or control over the underlying infrastructure. The vendor often commits to some level of service availability (measured in "uptime"—the percentage of business hours the service is available), with financial penalties for noncompliance.

For organizations with limited IT resources, the software-as-a-service model can be compelling. All of the headaches and variable costs associated with managing one's own infrastructure are eliminated, replaced with a constant, predictable monthly cost and a service that is available at any time and anywhere in the world where your staff has an Internet connection. However, some organizations may have privacy or security policies that may not permit hosting customer data outside of the corporate network.

This convenience comes with higher costs; over a typical application lifespan, software-as-a-service applications will typically have a higher total software cost than on-premises applications. Another critical factor to consider is a nonmonetary one; it is the loss of control associated with this type of application. Once you have years of historical data and trained users in a CRM application, you are in many ways "locked in." The transition at that point to another application can be extremely expensive. And yet, the SaaS provider may elect to change their terms or pricing in ways that you cannot now anticipate. When they do, this high switching cost will grant them enormous leverage in any subsequent negotiation. We have heard that getting out of a bad SaaS application can be compared to getting out of a bad marriage—often a messy, contentious, and expensive experience.

Application Access

The way that users interact with the CRM application is another consideration in evaluating CRM applications.

- *Client application*: This approach, where users install an application on their computers to access the CRM application, is disappearing from the CRM market, being replaced by web browser access and mobile device access. The key benefits of this form of access are the ability to have a richer application than is currently possible via a browser-based application (though web applications are catching up here quickly) and the ability to cache CRM data locally to allow for offline usage.

- *Web application*: This is the dominant approach to application access in today's CRM market. The CRM application is accessed via a secure web browser. The advantages are anywhere-access; CRM is available from any computer where an Internet connection can be made, and no software must be installed on the computer to access CRM. Deploying and maintaining this type of CRM application is also dramatically simpler, because no software must be installed, updated, or patched on the users' computers.

- *Mobile device access*: As handheld devices such as smartphones and tablets grow in power, flexibility, and prevalence, CRM access via mobile device is becoming more and more important. A well-designed mobile application can have a significant impact on user adoption by mobile workers, who often want to enter notes and set up meetings while visiting customers. They can also make use of the device features (for example, camera, GPS) to enable new scenarios, for example to generate directions to your customer's location.

- *Microsoft Outlook–integrated application*: Several CRM vendors offer either Outlook-integrated CRM client applications or add-ons to integrate CRM features into Microsoft Outlook. CRM users spend a large portion of their screen time working within Outlook, and it represents a primary tool for customer interaction. Several CRM user scenarios can be streamlined by building CRM features into Outlook, such as recording e-mail interactions and meetings with customers in CRM and creating new contact records.

Licensing Models

For readers new to the world of enterprise software, a number of different licensing models are in use, with implications for initial and ongoing costs of the software. Some of the ways in which these models vary is in what gets licensed, for what time period, for what kind of user, and for what kind of access. These variations are described next.

What Gets Licensed: Named User, Device, Connection...

Named user licensing refers to the model in which licenses are purchased and assigned to individual users; only these users are licensed to use the software, but they can do so using any computer or device they choose. This is perhaps the most common form of licensing.

Some software is licensed to a specific computer. This is common in a call center environment, where multiple shifts of users use the same set of computers at different times. The computer itself is licensed, regardless of how many different individuals use it.

Under concurrent licensing, the organization licenses a specific number of concurrent (that is, simultaneous) connections to the application server. This is typically managed by the server software, which will deny connections in excess of the number of concurrent licenses purchased. This model is useful where the software requires only occasional use but by a large group of users. Accounting software is often licensed in this manner; a ten-person accounting team may license only three or four concurrent licenses for the accounting package, because the users do not work constantly in the application but rather log in and out during the day as needed.

For How Long: Perpetual Licenses vs. Subscription Licensing

Perpetual licensing is the most familiar license term; it continues to be the dominant form of PC-based software licensing. As the name implies, purchasing a product under this model allows the user the right to use the software in perpetuity. Some important qualifiers typically apply; in most cases, a separate and recurring maintenance fee is required for access to technical support and to secure the right to install and use subsequent software versions. If a user elects not to pay the maintenance fees, future versions typically must be purchased at full price.

Subscription licensing is akin to a "rental" model. The user is entitled to use the software only for the subscription term. Typically technical support and upgrade rights are included in the subscription license without any additional fees.

Other Licensing Scenarios to Consider

A number of additional licensing scenarios exist that may be relevant for CRM software, and during an evaluation, one ought to understand how each relevant scenario is addressed by each vendor's license model. Some of these scenarios include the following.

End-Customer and Partner Access

Many business situations require nonemployees to access the CRM software in a controlled fashion. Two common examples illustrate this:

- The organization develops and implements a customer portal that is connected to their CRM application. This portal allows their customers to log in and view/enter data directly into the CRM application (for example, address updates, e-mail preferences, and customer support tickets).

- The organization develops and implements a partner portal that is connected to their CRM application. This portal allows them to distribute qualified sales leads to their channel partners and for the channel partners to provide updates on their sales efforts, to order marketing collateral, and to register their customers.

The relatively high cost of CRM licenses typically makes purchasing them for all customers and partners who would need CRM access in these scenarios cost-prohibitive. For this reason, many CRM vendors offer a special "External Access" or "External Connector" license, intended to allow nonemployees access to the CRM software at a reasonable cost.

Read-Only Access

Within an organization, in addition to the regular, transactional users of the CRM application, there may exist a set of users who need only to view information from the

CRM application and do not need to enter or edit this information. The common example here is the senior executive, who does not work directly with customers and does not have information to enter into CRM but who requires summary reporting from CRM and occasional read-only access.

Customers oppose purchasing full user licenses for these individuals, given their light usage profile, and many CRM vendors have responded by creating "read-only" or "reporting" licenses at dramatic discounts to the full licenses.

Selecting the Right CRM Software

CRM software selection can be a complex affair; the market is full of products that are branded "CRM" when in fact they vary widely in cost, functionality, complexity, architecture, and flexibility. Selecting the product that is right for your business can be a challenge and requires a well-thought-out process and a clear set of criteria against which to score candidate CRM applications.

Evaluation Criteria for CRM Applications

In this section, we will describe a set of criteria that you can use to evaluate how well a given CRM application is aligned to your organization's needs.

Alignment with Your Organization and Objectives

This is the most intuitive and fundamental of the criteria presented here. You need to evaluate how well a particular CRM application aligns with your organization and with your objectives and priorities, as defined in your own CRM roadmap. This criterion can be broken down further into a set of subcriteria:

- *Feature/function alignment:* If the source of your pain is in your service organization, don't select a sales-centric CRM application whose service functionality was added as an afterthought to "round out" the product. If your sales team is highly mobile, ensure the product you select has a mobile device platform that meets your needs.

- *Global-readiness alignment*: If your employees and customers are global, look hard at each product's multicurrency and multilanguage capabilities. How does it handle storing and updating exchange rates? What about value-added tax (VAT) and other international taxation issues? Global character sets? You might be surprised how many applications, designed for the American market, do not handle the double-byte characters needed for data entry in many languages. Inquire as to whether the application has been optimized for use in a wide-area network (WAN) environment between geographically dispersed offices.

- *Scalability alignment*: If your CRM community may grow to 1,000 or more users, look critically at each product's technology architecture with an eye to its scalability, and require each vendor to provide reference customers with a similar number of users. Many CRM applications were designed for individuals and small teams; success at this end of the market has led them to be pushed upmarket into larger and larger customers. Their development teams attempt to make the application suitable for these "enterprise" customers, but they cannot escape their product's underlying architecture, which is simply not appropriate for this scenario.

Customization Flexibility

Once you have selected a CRM application, your consulting partner will work with your organization through an implementation process to identify how CRM will be used to support your business; together you will identify changes to your business processes and to the CRM product to deliver the best possible solution. Once the solution is built, your users are trained, and you launch the solution into production, your team will be off and running, and your consulting partner's project team will fade out of the picture, off to help their next client.

Here is where the problems can potentially start. Your CRM has been designed to support your business as it operates today. However, the next new product area, new customer segment, new division, and new organizational structure for your business are not far in the future. If you can't evolve your CRM system to keep pace with your evolving business, you will find that it becomes less and less useful or relevant over time and provides less and less value to the organization. One option is to bring back your consulting partner to make changes to the system layout and behavior, but this might require long lead times to schedule resources, time to ramp the new team on your business, and costs. It is preferable that your internal team is able to develop some degree of self-sufficiency when it comes to reconfiguring and customizing the CRM solution.

Given this objective, some key questions for the CRM product include the following:

- What are the customization and configuration capabilities of the application?

- What tools are provided?

- What are the skills required for different types of customization?

- How are custom reports developed?

Then compare the answers to the skills of the members of your internal team, and the costs to acquire those skills if necessary in the marketplace, to get a sense of how feasible it will be for you to develop the capability to "evolve" the system without external support.

Alignment with Your Existing Infrastructure

This criterion is about evaluating potential applications not in isolation but rather in the context of your organization's existing customer data platform. What I mean by "customer data platform" is the existing systems that are used to store and process customer information, for example, your financial accounting system, your service management system, your customer portal website, your e-mail messaging system, and so on. CRM applications, because of their customer-centric nature, will need to integrate and interact with these other systems and so should be built around compatible software infrastructure where possible. This will allow you to develop these integrations with a minimum of difficulty and cost and will simplify the management of the customer data platform. The more different technologies at play within your environment, the more skills your IT team needs to master, which may translate into a larger team, impacting cost. For example, if you are an Oracle database shop running SAP for financial accounting and Lotus Notes for e-mail, Microsoft Dynamics CRM may not be the best choice for a CRM solution, because it runs on the SQL Server platform and integrates tightly with the Microsoft Outlook e-mail client.

The User Experience

Usability is a critically important factor in CRM solution evaluation. If you consider the chain of elements required for success in a CRM initiative, the user adoption link is often the weakest and the point at which may of these initiatives fail. To put it even more plainly, a poor user experience has doomed more CRM initiatives than perhaps any other factor. CRM strategies depend on the participation of every customer-facing employee; in most cases, the key role of these individuals is to provide information on their customers and their interactions to the rest of the organization, via data entry into the CRM application.

If the CRM application is difficult or time-consuming to use or learn, it will cause friction with the end users. This friction may eventually result in users abandoning the CRM solution, especially if either of the following is true:

- They see little direct benefit from its use.

- Yours is a culture where management is unable or unwilling to make CRM a required part of doing business.

Once this slide toward abandonment begins, it accelerates with a positive feedback effect. The less the end users contribute to the CRM solution, the less valuable the management reporting from the system becomes, and the less useful CRM becomes as a tool to monitor performance and team activity. This weakens management's enthusiasm and commitment to the tool, which makes it easier for end users to abandon the solution, and so on.

There are a number of strategies to prevent this situation and to ensure CRM adoption and success. Many are people and process strategies and are largely independent of the actual CRM application used. However, user adoption should definitely be a consideration in CRM software selection, and the key facilitators of adoption from an application standpoint are ease of use and the value it can deliver to end users. Some of what you are trying to understand about the application to gauge usability and end user value are the following:

- To deliver the outcomes that you require from CRM, what must each end-user role (salesperson, customer service person, marketing coordinator, and so on) do in the CRM application?

- How difficult/time-intensive is the solution to access and use? How many clicks and screens are required to accomplish the tasks identified in the previous item?

- How difficult will the solution be for users to learn? How similar is it to tools they already use or are already familiar with?

- Where does the solution provide value to the end user? Where does it accelerate or eliminate manual tasks or provide new insights that they do not have today? Is the CRM application a net "work-creator" or "work-reducer" for each end-user role?

If your evaluation of these questions is generally negative and it looks that CRM may be a net "work-creator" for many of your end users, you need to balance this with the value CRM adds to the business in other areas and carefully consider the likelihood of you being able to drive adoption of the tool despite this.

Technology Standards

This criterion has a lot in common with aligning with your existing infrastructure, but here, rather than comparing the CRM application's underlying technology to your existing infrastructure, you are trying to understand the extent it is built on industry-standard technology. If you spend enough time in technology consulting, you run across the horror stories of businesses that have held onto an aging application for too long or had one custom developed using arcane technology. They can't find any developers or consultants who understand it and can work with it. It is difficult or impossible to integrate with their other systems. Reporting tools cannot access it. It causes headaches in dozens of ways and can be onerously expensive to operate. In contrast, applications built on standard platforms—standard databases, standard programming languages, accessible with standards-compliant web services—are far easier to work with.

Vendor Viability and Ecosystem

The strength, commitment, and dynamism of the vendor behind your CRM application is an important selection criterion, because the life span of a CRM application is long, and changing CRM applications can be a complex and expensive endeavor. You want to select a vendor who is going to continue to invest in their CRM application, to develop innovative new features, to take advantage of new technologies, and to update their application as other products that it depends on are updated. So, be cautious when evaluating a vendor who is privately held (because their financial condition is difficult to judge), whose market share is flat or declining, who is not profitable, or who is new to the CRM market.

The vendor "ecosystem" refers to the community of supporting products and organizations that surround a CRM application. Elements of the ecosystem include the following:

- *Consulting partners:* Service firms with the skills and experience to install, configure, and customize the CRM application

- *Independent software vendors (ISVs):* Software companies that produce add-on or complementary products that enhance the CRM application's capabilities

- *Training firms:* Service firms that specialize in training users and administrators of the CRM application

- *User groups:* Associations, typically local, of customers who meet regularly to exchange best practices and share experiences using the CRM application

A dynamic, growing vendor and a thriving ecosystem tend to go hand in hand. A strong ecosystem will yield a better experience for you as a customer; with it, you will find a large and successful ISV community with a greater variety of products, a choice of several experienced local consulting partners, convenient training options, and an active community of customers to network with and learn from.

Cost

Understand the cost of acquiring and deploying the CRM application. This should be as inclusive a cost as possible—the relevant industry buzzword here is *total cost of ownership* (TCO). It's important to consider not only direct costs such as hardware, software licenses, and consulting but also the number and type of internal resources required to manage the application and their associated costs. These costs should be considered for a reasonable period of time; we typically recommend five to seven years.

The topic of cost would not be complete without a word about return on investment (ROI) analysis for CRM implementations. Frankly, it's probably not worth the trouble. A common desire on the part of organizations preparing to make an investment of the scale of a new CRM application is for an ROI analysis to describe the payback period for the CRM investment and the sources of the return on CRM. Often they will require the vendor to provide this or to assist in its construction. In our experience, this is almost always a waste of time, because the analysis is rarely credible. CRM is simply not a product that lends itself to easily quantifiable benefits. What is the dollar value of making a better business decision? What is the dollar value of new sales that will result from service staff sharing a system with the sales team and being able to easily alert them of opportunities? The analyst quickly finds themselves guessing at numbers, trying to figure out what sounds "reasonable" in order to quantify these benefits for the analysis (for example, "20 net new leads a month will be communicated to sales from the service department via the CRM application"). There are often a few quantifiable scenarios that can be included—often around streamlined reporting processes—but in the end these don't paint a complete picture.

There are investment choices for which a detailed and rigorous ROI analysis can inform decision making, but CRM application selection is not one of them.

The Software Evaluation Process

The process outlined in this section can be used to select the most appropriate CRM application for your organization from what is a crowded market. We will describe the process in detail, but a few key points are important to highlight before diving in:

- The foundation of the entire exercise is a thorough and thoughtful study of your organization's situation, plans, and needs. This work is typically encapsulated in the CRM roadmap described in Chapter 3. You can't choose the right application without understanding what "right" means for you.

- Throughout the process, it's important to use the same criteria and gather the same information for each product and vendor. The goal throughout is to facilitate an apples-to-apples comparison to the extent possible. Many vendors will "suggest" an evaluation process that is biased toward their product; if you end up using a different process for each, you will not be able to effectively compare and make a selection.

The CRM evaluation process involves the steps shown in Figure 4-1.

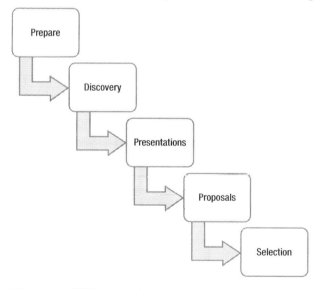

Figure 4-1. CRM application evaluation process

Preparing for the Evaluation

The following are the steps to prepare for the evaluation.

Identify Evaluation Team

Representatives of each stakeholder group should be members of the evaluation team; this would include managers from each business group who will use the new CRM application and a representative from the information technology group who can evaluate the application from a technical perspective. Ideally, the ultimate decision maker should be involved at this level, but in many situations this is not feasible.

Develop Evaluation Assessment Guide

This document describes all the specific items that require evaluation and will be used to assess and record how well each CRM application addresses each item. The exact structure is not important and should reflect your own situation and needs.

Table 4-1 describes a sample assessment guide. The document is organized as a table, with evaluation items organized by criteria area. For each item, there are columns to record the relative importance, how well the CRM application being evaluated addresses the item, and a notes section.

Table 4-1. Sample Assessment Guide

Eval Item	Importance	Score	Notes
Alignment with Objectives			
Manage Lead Import and Qualification			
Easy path exists to import leads from Excel into the application.	Medium		
Application supports lead segmentation and qualification.	Medium		
Application can categorize leads based on where they are in the sales cycle.	High		
Application facilitates handoff of qualified leads from inside sales to field sales organization without dropping them.	Medium		

Eval Item	Importance	Score	Notes
Support Field Sales Process			
Application supports activity tracking associated with opportunities.	High		
Application supports structured sales process, with gates and hard-coded close probabilities.	High		
Provide Sales Visibility to Management			
Application allows sales activities to be organized by sales territories in a three-level hierarchy.	High		
Application can display a sales dashboard that shows real-time sales pipeline by sales rep, territory, customer segment, and sales stage. Can be weighted by sales stage, close probability, or sales representative's confidence.	High		
Application contains alerting capabilities for large/strategic deals.	Low		
Improve Field Sales Productivity			
Application eliminates need for sales reps to prepare a forecast report.	High		
Helps sales reps organize their daily activities, such as e-mails, calls, and so on.	Medium		
Helps sales reps collaborate with sales engineers, product engineering, sales management.	Medium		
Sales reps can create/update customers, activities, and opportunities from a mobile device.	High		

Eval Item	Importance	Score	Notes
Global-Readiness Alignment			
Application is available in both English and Spanish.	Low		
Application allows the use of multiple currencies and allows for management of exchange rates.	Medium		
Scalability Alignment			
Application can scale to support 200 users.	High		
Customization Flexibility			
Application schema can be extended to define new system entities.	High		
Custom logic can be added to execute when system events occur (for example, a customer is created, a lead is qualified).	High		
Application includes user-focused tools for custom report generation.	Medium		
Application allows complex custom reports to be developed and published.	High		
System architecture prevents custom logic from complicating the version upgrade process.	Medium		
Application allows organization to define workflow processes to automate common tasks (for example, approval processes) and improve communication (for example, auto e-mail notifications when certain events occur).	Medium		

Alignment with Customer Infrastructure			
Packaged integration available to our accounting system.	Medium		
Application database platform is the same as our accounting and provisioning applications.	High		
Both client and server (if exists) run on Windows.	High		
The User Experience			
How easy is it for a rep to enter a new contact into CRM?	High		
How easy is it for a rep to log a customer call or meeting into CRM?	High		
How easy is it for a rep to enter and update their sales opportunities?	High		
Application is accessible from any Internet connection without the need to make a VPN connection.	Medium		
How easy is it for a sales rep to access a list of upcoming activities, such as meetings, calls, tasks?	High		
Technology Standards			
Application uses a standard database platform.	High		
Application has a web services API to facilitate integration.	High		
Custom application logic can be written with standard programming language and tools.	High		
Application can be supported by a standard disaster recovery plan.	High		

Vendor Viability and Ecosystem			
The vendor's CRM customer base is significant and/or growing.	High		
CRM is a core product of the company and has a place in its long-term strategy.	High		
There is a healthy community of ISVs actively developing products for this platform.	Medium		
Vendor is profitable.	High		

Cost Assessment

The different licensing models used by CRM vendors can sometimes make apples-to-apples comparisons challenging. The best approach is to define a standard cost framework and then enlist each vendor in completing it for their application. Table 4-2 gives a sample template, but you should adjust it as needed for your situation.

Table 4-2. Sample Cost Assessment

Cost Element	Year 1	Year 2	Year 3	Year 4	Year 5	Year 6	Year 7
Server hardware including operating systems and database software	$20,000	$0	$0	$0	$20,000	$0	$0
CRM software licenses for 100 users, maintenance, and technical support	$100,000	$20,000	$20,000	$20,000	$20,000	$20,000	$20,000
System maintenance/administration	$80,000	$80,000	$80,000	$80,000	$80,000	$80,000	$80,000
Consulting assistance	$90,000	$30,000	$0	$0	$0	$40,000	$0
TOTAL THIS YEAR	$290,000	$130,000	$100,000	$100,000	$120,000	$140,000	$100,000
TOTAL SINCE INCEPTION	$290,000	$420,000	$520,000	$620,000	$740,000	$880,000	$980,000

The following are some notes on the template:

- "Server hardware" is relevant for on-premises CRM applications that require installation on servers in your own data center. The repeating cost in year 5 represents a periodic hardware upgrade.

- The "CRM software licenses" row represents the total costs to the CRM software vendor, excluding implementation.

- "System maintenance/administration" attempts to summarize the costs associated with keeping the CRM application running. For example, if a full-time administrator will be needed, the cost of this resource needs to be factored into the analysis. This is a difficult factor to estimate precisely, but a few guidelines may be helpful. Software-as-a-service vendors typically have lower costs in this area, because there is no server management (patching, backing up, and recovering from disasters) associated with this model. However, the majority of administration costs are related to user support, reporting support, and business analysis, which are independent of deployment method. In general, a useful budgeting rule of thumb is to budget for 0.25–0.5 of an FTE for a small CRM deployment (as measured in users/scope), one to three FTEs for a medium deployment, and four to eight FTEs for a large deployment.

- Consulting assistance is included in year 1 for the initial implementation and at a smaller level in year 2. Typically some kind of support agreement with your consulting partner is useful in the first year or two, because your internal team is still ramping up on the application. If you are dedicating internal resources to administer and manage CRM, we would expect the need for this support to taper off, though you may still engage your partner for significant development efforts or CRM version upgrades (which is the reason for the additional $40,000 in consulting assistance in year 6).

Identify and Research Potential Vendors

There are a number of potential methods to identify potential vendors and CRM applications and to narrow this field to a select few for full evaluation. The following are some sources of information about CRM applications and vendors:

- *Analyst reports*: The major technology analyst firms (Gartner, Forrester, Aberdeen, and so on) cover the CRM market and release regular reports detailing the vendors in the market and their comparative strengths, weaknesses, and prospects. Often these reports are made available by the featured vendors themselves.

- *The CRM press*: There are several CRM-focused business journals.

- *Peer networking and industry groups*: These are a great place not only to understand what applications other businesses are using but to get a feel for how satisfied the customers of different vendors are in their applications.

- *User groups*: The larger vendors in terms of market share are likely to have active user groups in your area. Most of these groups will welcome prospective customers attending a meeting, and it can be a good place to get an "unfiltered" perspective on the product.

- *Financial reports*: If the vendors you are researching are publicly traded, their annual reports can provide insight into the health of their business and their strategic direction.

- *CRM conferences*: Although attending can be expensive, for a short list of vendors, attending their customer conference can be extremely educational. There will be many opportunities to learn about the product, to hear from customers about their successes and frustrations, and to see the vendor ecosystem in full display.

The objective of this initial research is to whittle down the CRM market to a "short list" of two to three applications to evaluate fully.

The Discovery Phase

The objective of the discovery phase is to educate the vendors on your organization and your needs, to equip them explain and demonstrate how their application will meet your specific requirements, and to gain an overview level of familiarity with each vendor's application.

Some people have a tendency to treat the customer-vendor relationship as inherently adversarial and are reluctant to share detailed information about their situation and objectives. In our experience, this perspective is not helpful. It forces the vendor into a generic presentation that is of limited value and puts an unfair share of the work in evaluating whether the application is a fit on the customer, when it should be shared with the vendor. The discovery process is bidirectional; the vendor is learning about the customer's needs and what information they need to provide to support the evaluation, and the customer is learning the details of the vendor and the application.

Each vendor is likely to have their own methodology for gathering your CRM requirements, and there is little harm in letting each structure the process in their own way. One approach that you can offer is "job shadowing" with users in key roles who would be users of the CRM application, where the vendor sits with these users and observes their activities and how the current tools support them.

The important tasks for customers in this phase are to do the following:

- Give each vendor a thorough overview of the business and the drivers behind the CRM initiative.

- Walk each vendor through the evaluation guide so that they are clear on what needs they must address in their presentation and demonstrations.

- Ensure that the same information is communicated to each.

Plan to make subject-matter experts from the evaluation team and potentially your CRM executive sponsor available to meet with vendors during this phase. Vendors will likely want to meet with these individuals to ask clarifying questions on your situation. Preparing a detailed, customized presentation and demonstration is a time-intensive effort on the part of the vendors; they will want to do everything they can to ensure that their understanding of the situation and the levers that will drive selection are complete. The number of meetings required to complete discovery will vary with the scope and complexity of your organization and CRM needs; a small business with a single location that just needs a tool to import and qualify leads will require a simpler process than a global enterprise seeking to roll out an integrated sales, marketing, and customer service application to hundreds or thousands of users.

Vendor Presentations

This is the time in the process when each vendor makes their formal pitch as to how their solution would address your needs, why it is superior to the competition, and what the costs are likely to be. Schedule presentations with enough lead time to allow each vendor to develop a quality presentation that speaks to your organization's requirements, and don't schedule more than one vendor per day; these sessions can be draining for all parties involved. Here are a few guidelines to make the most of the vendor presentations:

- Insist that the vendor clearly identify which elements of any demonstration are standard functionality and which were third-party add-ons or custom developed afterward, either specifically for the demo or for a customer. For custom development items, inquire as to the approximate development effort involved.

- Insist that each vendor demonstrate the key user experience scenarios. If the scenarios are standard functionality, they should be able to show how they would be completed in the application.

- Make sure you leave the presentation with the evaluation guide and cost assessment complete.

The Follow-up Phase

After completing the vendor presentations and debriefing with your internal team, you will ideally be able to rank the potential applications based on their performance against your evaluation criteria and their cost. The primary next step is checking references. Also, at this point, if the vendor has not already introduced an implementation partner, you will want to solicit their recommendation for local firms with good track records of delivering successful projects. We will cover evaluation of consulting partners later in this chapter.

Reference checking is an important part of the evaluation process. Request two to four reference customers, either in your industry or with similar customer-facing processes. Although local customers are appealing for the prospect of meeting face-to-face and seeing the application "in action," location is less important than finding reference customers that most closely match your organization. Thoughtful preparation will allow you to get the most from the reference meeting and to make the best use of the reference's time. Here are a number of suggested questions/topics for this discussion:

- Implementation experience
  - What was the scope of the initial implementation project?
  - How long did the project take?
  - What did it cost? Were there cost overruns? How were these communicated to you?
  - What went smoothly, and what was challenging?
  - What surprised you about the application?
- User adoption

- How successful has adoption of the application by users been?

- What application areas cause the most friction for users?

- Costs

    - How many FTEs in what roles are needed to support and administer the application?

- Overall experience

    - If you had the decision to make again, would you choose this application again?

Selection

The combination of the completed evaluation guides, cost assessments, and reference reports for the short-listed applications should allow for a clear ranking. If your partner evaluation was conducted concurrently with your application evaluation, as is often the case, the strength of the partners for each application should certainly be a factor as well. Contract negotiation follows selection.

Variation: Site Visit

A variation on the reference check is the site visit, where the vendor coordinates a visit at an existing customer location. This allows for more detailed discussions with a wider variety of roles (users, managers, administrators, and IT) and the opportunity to job shadow and see the application in action.

Variation: Pilots and Proof-of-Concept Projects

In some situations, it is judged to be an unacceptable risk to select and implement a CRM application using the process outlined earlier. A pilot or proof-of-concept can further validate that a selected application will meet the organization's goals but will require additional budget and will delay a decision and implementation.

A *proof-of-concept* typically involves installing a trial version of the application and investing sufficient consulting budget to configure the application to explore and validate the highest-risk scenarios. The application is never used for production data.

A *pilot* refers to a limited-scope but complete implementation to assess the application in production, with a subset of users. For example, a company may implement CRM to a small subsidiary or to a specific geographic location as a pilot before deciding whether to roll it out organization-wide.

With both the pilot and the proof-of-concept, the objective is to enable a decision that the organization cannot make with the information it currently has. For these efforts to be of any value, it must be clearly mapped out beforehand how the results will lead to a decision. The following are some of the key questions: What must be demonstrated to enable a "go" decision on the larger project? Can this be objectively measured, and if so, how? If not, whose interpretation will be used for the decision?

Selecting the Right Consultants

Evaluating consulting partners is significantly simpler than applications. As with application evaluation, there are a number of criteria to be considered. Before considering criteria, however, you may be asking yourself a more fundamental question: do I even need consultants? The CRM vendors spend significant marketing energy emphasizing the ease of use of their applications and the speed with which they can be deployed. Demonstrations make configuration look like simple exercises in point-and-click. Can't we just do this ourselves and save a lot of money?

As individuals who have built careers helping organizations find success with CRM, you could argue that our answer to this question is not credibly objective, but we believe passionately in the value consultants provide. Here are a few specific examples of what a consulting partner can bring to the table:

- Deep technical skill and experience with the specific CRM application. A consulting partner can help design the optimal solution for your business needs by understanding all the CRM application's features and platform capabilities and how best to harness them to solve your particular business problem. In addition, configuration and development work can be completed by a consulting partner far more quickly; in most cases, they are not "learning as they go" and can also often leverage a library of prebuilt solutions from past engagements.

- Deep understanding of the process of implementing CRM, including how to conduct requirements and design meetings effectively, how to manage development and test environments, how to migrate data into CRM, and how best to train field sales reps...to call out a few examples. It may be that no one in your organization has ever done this before.

- A wealth of experience in how successful organizations use CRM applications, including how they have meshed their processes and their chosen application to deliver the best customer experience or to streamline their operations.

CRM is typically a significant investment on the part of the organization; using a quality consulting partner is a risk mitigator that can help ensure that a return is realized on that significant investment.

Evaluation Criteria

Evaluating consultants is typically a simpler task than software. The following criteria will help you make an informed choice of partner for your CRM initiative.

Experience Implementing the CRM Application

The most obvious criteria is a partner's experience with your selected application. Ideally, the partner should have several years' experience with the application, spreading across a number of individual consultants on their team. If the CRM vendor offers a certification program for partners, inquire as to each partner's level within the program.

As the scope of your project is defined, inquire as to the potential partner's experience and proficiency in each project element. For example, if you will require a custom component, understand the partner's programming staff's experience and depth. If you require integration to any existing line-of-business applications, what integration tool would your partner recommend, and when have they successfully deployed such an integration?

Experience with Your Industry

A successful CRM implementation project is a two-way education; you are learning about the application from your partner, and to be effective, they must learn about you and your business. If the partner has worked with organizations in your industry, they will have a leg up in their education.

Experience with Your Organization Scale

Different sized organizations present different challenges to successful CRM implementations. Risk areas, business scenarios, and implementation methodologies change with organization scale. Don't expect a small business partner to be able to operate successfully at the enterprise level or an enterprise-level partner to be able to adapt and adjust to small-business needs.

Staffing Plan and Project Management Methodology

Make sure you understand each partner's staffing plan for your project. How many consultants, playing what roles? How many other projects would these consultants work on at the same time? The ideal situation is to have dedicated resources; it's a serious red flag if any partner asks their people to juggle more than two projects simultaneously. The complexity of CRM projects makes it very difficult to effectively manage the schedule, configuration, and requirements of multiple clients simultaneously. Corners invariably get cut.

Understand a potential partner's project management methodology. Look for a methodology that accomplishes the following:

- Keeps the customer informed as to project progress and budget status

- Prevents "surprise" project overages

- Includes review and approval milestones at appropriate points in the project to keep things from going off track

- Prepares your internal team to administer CRM once the project is complete

Location

Technology is making it easier for remote workers to participate in a project without the historical communications problems and related productivity loss associated with geographically dispersed project teams. There are, however, some considerations associated with engaging a partner who either is not local or plans to assign remote resources to your project.

Some project roles lend themselves to remote work. Development and testing work can often be accomplished successfully by remote workers, though we recommend dedicating extra time to ensure that specifications are sufficiently detailed, because a remote developer inherently has less of a feel for the customer's needs than one that is on-site and sitting in business process and design meetings.

We caution against trying to execute the process analysis and application design project components with remote resources; these parts of the project are when the two-way education we described earlier takes place, and this is best accomplished face-to-face. There is no substitute for time spent together in a conference room with a whiteboard.

So for remote partners, ensure that they plan to have their analysts and design roles work on-site and understand the costs associated with this, because travel costs are passed on to the customer.

Cost

Consulting costs to implement CRM vary widely with the scope of these projects, from the small or mid-market business looking to roll out a foundation of basic CRM capabilities to support their planned growth to large enterprises requiring complex integrations and multisource data migrations. A rough rule of thumb that scales with the complexity of your organization is to expect a 1:0.75 to 1:2 ratio of software to services costs.

Reference Checks for Consulting Partners

Checking references for consulting partners is as important as for CRM application vendors. As with the vendors, try to speak with two to four reference clients for each potential partner, and aim for the best match to your organization and the scope of your project.

In addition to their general performance and the client's satisfaction with them, some of the specific areas to drill into with consulting partner references are as follows:

- *Consistency of the team*: Some consulting organizations treat projects, especially larger ones, as "revolving doors," cycling consultants on and off regularly as competing projects require staffing or consultants wrap up other projects in an effort to provide short project start lead times to other clients and to maintain high utilization. These resource changes can be disruptive and inefficient, because new resources must be ramped up and departing resources invariably take some information with them. Avoid partners for whom this is the norm and not the exception. In a related point, inquire about the tenure of consultants with the organization. High turnover can be a red flag of problems with the organization that may impact your project.

- *Budget performance.* CRM consulting engagements are typically structured on a time-and-materials basis, which means that the project does not have a built-in cost "cap" as a fixed-fee or not-to-exceed arrangement would. The time-and-materials approach is necessary because the project cannot be sufficiently defined at the outset to allow the consulting partner to offer a fixed fee without having to include such a large margin of safety as to make the project cost unacceptably high. The result, however, is that a consulting partner's budget performance is a very important thing to understand. Some consulting partners have a tendency to underbid to win projects; knowing how a partner has performed against their budget estimates in the past should help assess what their likely true costs will be and plan accordingly.

- *Documentation and knowledge transfer.* Months after your CRM engagement, you may need to change the way a piece of custom logic functions, modify a training document, or revisit how information is being integrated between your CRM application and other business applications. A good partner will have left behind a meticulous, well-organized set of documents that describe the application and the work they performed, and they will have walked one or more members of your staff through it. A poor partner will leave behind a scant assortment of documents, some complete, some incomplete, that may force you to play the detective to figure out how your application works and why it was developed as it was.

Final Thoughts

The CRM selection process can be overwhelming and daunting. Ideally this chapter has relieved some stress by outlining a methodical procedure to arrive at a selection. It all begins with your CRM roadmap, followed by the thoughtful development of your evaluation guide. Once this guide is complete, it becomes your touchstone to stay focused on what is important and avoid being distracted by the flash and sizzle of vendor demonstrations and presentations.

CHAPTER 5

Planning the Initial CRM Implementation

Through this point in the book, we have discussed some of the items that will dramatically impact the success of your CRM program. Keeping the components of a successful CRM program in mind as you and your team work through the initial stages of a CRM implementation will allow you to focus on the task at hand.

In this chapter, we will be concentrating on planning the first-phase implementation of your CRM program. We will walk you through the typical phases of an implementation, focus on dividing the available work, and talk through some of the detailed items that can make or break your implementation. More specifically, we are going to focus on concepts that should be evaluated or completed before the project begins. Although many of the concepts are not related to each other, it will be vital to evaluate each high-level item. They are all important when trying to effectively plan your initiative. We will provide overviews of the concepts shown in Figure 5-1.

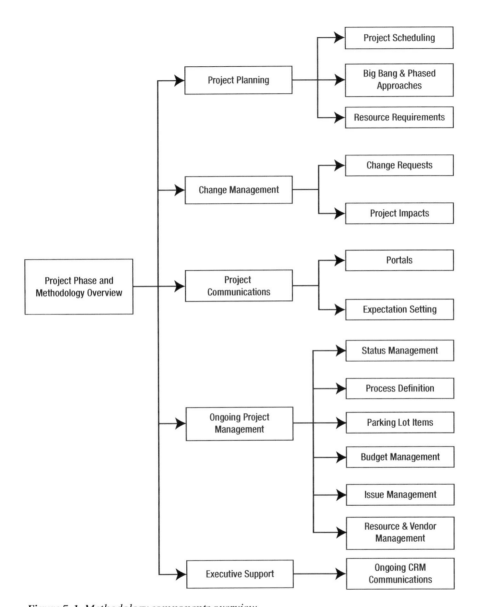

Figure 5-1. Methodology components overview

Finally, as we discussed in Chapter 3, ensuring that your CRM roadmap is always in mind as you work through the tasks and documents in this chapter will help guide you and answer any questions that arise.

Managing CRM Projects

Executing the initial phase of your CRM program will require you to balance a disciplined approach to project management and analysis with the flexibility needed to accommodate end users and ensure ultimate value for them. Much of the groundwork needed to maintain a disciplined approach was completed when you developed your CRM roadmap. The rest can be completed during the initial stage of the implementation.

At this point, it is important to review the difference between your CRM roadmap or program and a specific project or phase. The implementation in this chapter is specific to the project. Typically, a project will have defined start and end dates and will deliver a finite set of functionality to the end users. Each project will be a piece of a larger roadmap or program.

In the next section, we will begin to give you an overview of the things that make up a project. Initially, we will provide you with an overview of the typical stages of an implementation.

Understanding the Phases of a Project

Dozens of high-level methodologies exist and are commonly used for implementing technology applications. From the beginning, many organizations have a preference for a methodology, and frankly, most can be used or adapted for your CRM program. Based on our experience implementing CRM applications, we will provide some information on the most commonly used and successful methodologies and will recommend a process that ultimately takes the best from a number of approaches. This will provide you with something you can use as you implement the application in your organization.

The Software Development Life Cycle (SDLC)

The SDLC is a high-level process and set of associated tasks used for creating or altering systems. The methodologies outlined later in this chapter all utilize some parts of a classic SDLC process, so there will be an opportunity to leverage different pieces as you look for the best practices of each when working through your implementation. That said, they all tend to differ in how quickly you work through the various tasks, their flexibility when it comes to task completeness vs. moving on, and the level of detail they encourage you to track and utilize. The general components of a SDLC are as follows:

Plan/analyze: The plan/analyze activity, often also referred to as the *envisioning stage,* is the place where the goals of the project are outlined, the project ROI is defined, and the roles and responsibilities are identified for the phase of the implementation. This activity is also where the design of the application is completed and requirements are gathered, vetted, reviewed with the team, and finalized in some form. This design can take a number of approaches, some variants of which will be identified in the upcoming text, but ultimately, at the end of this phase, the requirements for the implementation phase have been identified and locked in.

Implementation: The implementation activity focuses on building any in-scope items identified during the plan/analyze stage of the implementation. During this activity of the SDLC, items are also unit tested, and bugs are fixed as necessary. Depending on the design approach you choose to take, the build phase may require more or less time, but ultimately, the development of the application will be complete when this phase ends. A number of very critical components of the implementation, including the various types of testing, need to be completed at this point as well. We will focus more on the various testing types later in this chapter.

Deploy and support: Deployment activities focus on rolling out the application to end users and supporting it after release. It is during this piece of the implementation that both end user and administrator training occur. The application is then rolled out to end users and appropriately supported following deployment.

Much of Chapter 6 will focus on providing additional detail on the previous items. Specifics about design, development, testing, training, and deployment will be outlined. For this chapter, now that we have identified the high-level activities to be completed as part of an implementation, we will provide additional detail on the various ways to implement these activities.

Waterfall Methodology

One of the most common methodologies used during technology and, more specifically, CRM implementations is the Waterfall methodology. This methodology is designed as a series of consecutive steps, one following the other, where the stages flow much like a waterfall. Figure 5-2 shows a simple, graphical example of a Waterfall methodology.

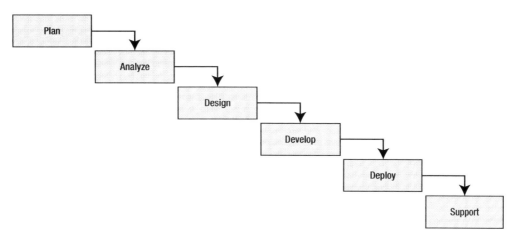

Figure 5-2. Waterfall methodology

Of primary importance to the Waterfall methodology is sequence. Generally, one step must be 100 percent complete prior to taking on the next. Additionally, this methodology is very heavily focused on documentation. The rigid structure of the Waterfall methodology often causes problems for implementation teams. A CRM project rarely moves in a straight line, so an ability to be creative and adapt project schedules to meet the team's needs is important. The heavy focus on documentation also puts a significant burden on the project team. Stakeholders are often stretched thin with their "day jobs" to begin with, so adding the weight of detailed documentation frequently causes all their work to suffer.

Scrum Methodology

Another common methodology is Scrum. The primary premise of this methodology is short, fixed-length design and development cycles. Scrum cycles typically range from two to four weeks and include very fixed scope. These cycles are often referred to as *sprints.* Each sprint begins with a discussion where the collected list of desired features is reviewed by the project team. The team then identifies the features that can successfully be developed within the two- to four-week sprint period, and then the work begins.

One key premise to the Scrum methodology is that once a sprint has been identified, it cannot be changed. That said, another key principle is flexibility. Because sprints are short in duration, the user community can more easily change their mind or approach to a requirement and can implement that change in a subsequent sprint. Items identified as features for the next sprint are called the *sprint backlog.*

Even though they're short, many of the activities identified in the SDLC are used, albeit in an abbreviated fashion. A brief design and development phase is followed by a demonstration of the new functionality. This demonstration replaces the more detailed training activity that occurs in longer projects. By nature, the project teams using the Scrum methodology meet regularly and briefly cover any items discussed in the plan/analyze phases through the life of a sprint. As an organization, Figure 5-3 shows how you might view a project that includes a number of sprints.

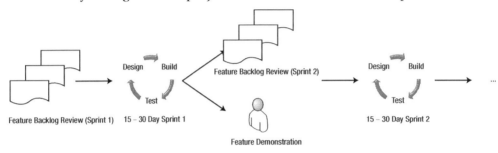

Figure 5-3. Scrum methodology

Iterative Development Methodology

Both of the methodologies outlined thus far have some limitations when associated with CRM implementations. Based on our experience, one of the biggest places where implementations can fail is a lack of user buy-in. One of the challenges with the Waterfall methodology is that the need to complete one stage before beginning the next requires the project team to develop a very detailed design document. This document is developed with input from the end users and reviewed prior to the beginning of development. Ultimately, the next time the user community will see the application is during user acceptance testing, so this approach opens the door for users to be surprised or disappointed with some of the assumptions or trade-offs made.

Many CRM implementations include enough functionality that short design sessions and quick development cycles associated with the Scrum approach make meeting users' expectations for an initial implementation difficult. Even the smallest of CRM implementations may take a number of weeks, with larger implementations taking 6 to 12 months or more. Additionally, one key premise of Scrum projects is a brief demonstration of new functionality to users instead of a full user training cycle. With most initial implementations, spending a significant amount of time educating users about the application, including where it can help them be more efficient in their jobs, is important.

Because of these and other limitations associated with many methodologies, we often employ a derivative of the iterative development methodology on our projects. This methodology is often referred to as the *iterative and incremental development methodology*. With this methodology, the idea is to loop your application through a repetitive (iterative) design process over a shorter period of time (incremental). Visually, this methodology looks very similar to the Waterfall methodology with two key differences:

- There is an overlap between stages when using the iterative development methodology. Much of the work to be completed in a particular stage can be started prior to the end of the previous stage.

- During the design phase, the iterative approach provides the implementation team with a mechanism to gather requirements, build or configure pieces of the application, and then repeat the process. The implementation team can repeat these iterations as many times as necessary to get the appropriate amount of feedback from the users.

Figure 5-4 shows how the iterative and incremental development methodology differs from the Waterfall methodology identified earlier in this chapter.

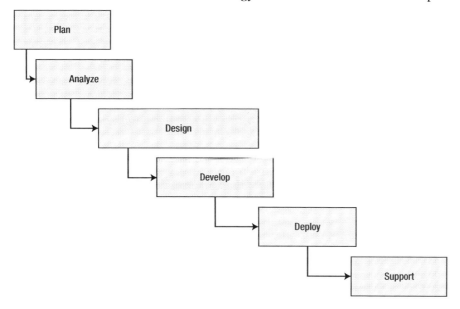

Figure 5-4. Iterative methodology

As you can see from Figure 5-4, the stages overlap, allowing tasks from one stage to begin before another is completed. The design stage of this methodology is typically longer than others because of the iterations. Additionally, you may typically see a shorter pure development stage because some development and configuration is being completed during the design stage. The iterative process should look like Figure 5-5.

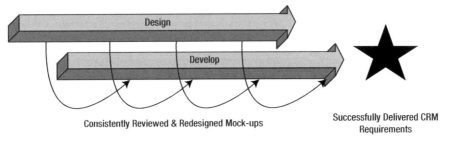

Figure 5-5. Iterative design and development

The iterative process should involve getting an application in front of end users quickly. Doing this will ensure the following:

- *User buy-in*: Engaging users through the application will allow them to become more invested in the end result. Additionally, because of the extended design timeline, the momentum of the project should continue through the end.

- *Accurate requirement capture*: The iterative process provides users and the implementation team with the opportunity to review and change the requirements multiple times prior to them being locked down. Instead of building a design document and hoping that it accurately captures the requirements, this approach allows users to see the end result even before that end result is completely defined.

- *Design and build consistency*: Having these two stages overlap so much provides additional consistency and checkpoints throughout the development process.

As we stated at the beginning of this section, many organizations have a methodology in place that they frequently use for technology implementations. That approach is fine as long as you make sure you adjust that methodology to provide users with the ability to see the application early and often.

Calculating ROI

Calculating and measuring ROI for a CRM project can be a challenging task. Rarely does an organization have the ability to successfully measure before and after metrics for things such as employee productivity or effectiveness. Often, the inability to measure those items is a large reason behind the implementation. That said, for the benefit of the organizations leadership team and to assist with messaging for the users, it is important to identify a couple of items to track and report on following deployment.

To ensure you cover this completely, you may want to devote some time prior to the deployment to identify the important items to track so that you can ultimately ensure that the project is successful.

Project Planning

The first step in choosing the appropriate approach for managing the schedule and associated items during the project is to identify the initial project schedule and milestones. Project planning as a concept includes not only managing the schedule but also managing associated resources and tasks.

Regardless of which project planning approach you choose, you should consider providing a high-level set of project milestones with an overall status of the milestones for the larger user community. Although those on the project team will value a more detailed set of tasks and dates, some may prefer a simple status outlining whether the project is on track and, if there are issues, how serious they are.

Project Scheduling

You might choose to approach the scheduling of your project and associated tasks in a number of ways. Table 5-1 shows an extremely simple example of something you could use.

Table 5-1. Milestone Summary

Milestone	Milestone Date	Status
Design Complete	17-Jun-11	On Schedule
Development Complete	29-Jul-11	Not Started
Testing Complete	9-Sep-11	Mitigated Risk
Training Complete	16-Sep-11	Significant Risk
Go-Live	26-Sep-11	
Post Go-Live Support Complete	5-Oct-11	

For the core project team, in addition to summarizing the milestones, you may choose to produce a simple or more complex project plan. For the simple plan, a spreadsheet-like tool easily allows you to customize the plan to accommodate requests from the team. At a minimum with this approach, you will want to track the following:

- *Tasks*: Focus in this model on identifying the tasks that are key to the project's success. These may be tasks that are high profile, tasks requiring significant resource coordination, or tasks that involve significant risk to the overall project.

- *Dates*: With a simple model, tracking the start and end dates will give people an idea of when a specific task is going to occur. You may also choose to identify key dates requiring significant involvement from subject-matter experts (SMEs) or others not on the core project team.

- *Resources*: Identifying the parties involved in the execution of a task will enable the collective project team to get on the same page about high-level task ownership.

- *SME time commitments*: One question that comes up regularly during projects is, "How much time will be required from my SMEs during certain phases?" Providing them with this information during the planning stage of the project will enable them to plan their time and will ensure the project team receives the necessary amount of time during the implementation.

Figure 5-6 shows a spreadsheet-based example of how to track these items.

Task	Start Date	End Date	Involved Parties	SME Time Commitment
Application Design & Configuration	9-May-11	17-Jun-11	SMEs, Consultant, IT	~6 hour per week
Application View Development	6-Jun-11	17-Jun-11	SMEs, Consultant, IT	~1 hour per week
Data Migration	13-Jun-11	1-Jul-11	IT	Minimal
Integration	13-Jun-11	15-Jul-11	IT	N/A
Report Development	13-Jun-11	15-Jul-11	IT	N/A
Custom Development	20-Jun-11	8-Jul-11	Consultant	N/A
Template (WM & Email) Development	11-Jul-11	22-Jul-11	Consultant, IT	~1 hour per week
3rd Party Product Installation & Configuration	11-Jul-11	29-Jul-11	Consultant, IT	N/A
System Testing	8-Aug-11	17-Aug-11	Consultant	N/A
Integration Testing	15-Aug-11	19-Aug-11	IT	N/A
User Acceptance Testing	22-Aug-11	2-Sep-11	SMEs, Consultant	~ 5 hours per week
Bug Fixes / Regression Testing	5-Sep-11	9-Sep-11	Consultant, IT	N/A
End User Training	12-Sep-11	16-Sep-11	SMEs, Consultant	~4 - 6 hours
Administrator Training	12-Sep-11	16-Sep-11	Consultant	N/A
Production Migration	19-Sep-11	21-Sep-11	Consultant, IT	N/A
Go-Live	21-Sep-11	26-Sep-11	SMEs, Consultant, IT	
Go-Live Support	26-Sep-11	5-Oct-11	Consultant, IT	N/A

Figure 5-6. High-level project schedule

This high-level approach is great for smaller projects or organizations that have a great understanding of classic SDLC activities and processes. For projects of more complexity or teams requiring additional information during the project, you should consider a more complex project planning process.

A number of tools can be used to manage more complex project tasks. One tool commonly used is Microsoft Project software. These tools allow you to manage information in addition to that listed for the simple solution, such as the following:

- *Detailed resource tracking*: Using one of the many complex tools available allows you to associate specific resources to specific tasks.

- *Resource leveling*: Most of these applications will also assist the project manager with resource leveling. Reports typically exist that that provide an overview of over-allocated resources within a specific period.

- *Milestone and tasks*: Unlike the simple formats, most of the complex PM tools provide you with the ability to track detailed tasks and high-level milestones in one document. Users can then choose to view the appropriate level of detail based on their role.

- *Task status*: Each task in a classic project plan also has an attribute associated with it that allows you to track status or percent complete. In the sample project plan displayed in Figure 5-7, the Draft Functional Design task has a black line in it showing how much of that task has been completed.

- *Project baselining*: A nice feature of complex project management tools is the ability to easily slide task start or end dates, and to have the other, subsequent tasks move as well. A downside to this approach is you lose the history of original dates. Because of this, many project planning tools allow you to baseline the project, thereby freezing the initial dates. Any updates are then tracked against that baseline. Figure 5-7 is an example of a complete project plan.

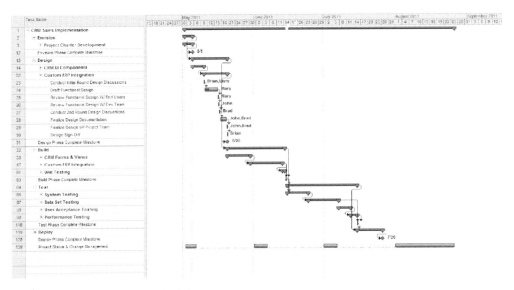

Figure 5-7. Detailed project schedule

Other items for you to include in your project plan, and ultimately the project charter document, are any project dependencies that exist related to this project. Clearly, seeing overlap in projects and resource assignments will allow you to mitigate risk up front in the process.

Big Bang vs. Phased Approach

One of the items that will have the biggest impact on the initial phase of your project is whether your organization takes a big bang or a phase approach to the implementation. Ultimately, this decision should be made well before you begin the first phase based on the roadmap you defined very early in the process. That said, many organizations are tempted to overlook the roadmap when scope presents itself during an initial phase. Here is a quick overview of the two approaches:

- *Big bang*: The big-bang approach typically includes significantly more scope than any phased approach. Often, multiple user groups (sales, service, and marketing, for example) will be included in the same implementation. A big-bang type of project usually includes some reporting, necessary integrations, and other items that allow the organization to see only small items remaining for future phases.

- *Phased*: A phased approach involves breaking key scope items into different phases to reduce risk and allow the user community to adapt to a single set of functions per phase. When a phased approach is utilized, things such as reporting, integrations, and custom code are often scheduled for a later phase to reduce the risk during the initial phase. Phasing also ensures that items built are needed based on user interaction with the application instead of based on some initial, high-level design.

Based on our experience implementing CRM programs, we typically recommend that customers utilize a phased approach. User adoption is typically higher, risk for the initial few phases is lower, and we have less "throwaway" code because what's built in later phases is defined by user needs when they're using the application instead of early design discussions.

Identifying Resource Requirements

After you have documented all the tasks that need to occur on a project, you can begin identifying the appropriate resources needed for the job. As we discussed in Chapter 4, these resource could come from many sources and have many different focuses. Spending the time to identify these up front is critical to the project's success.

Identifying Critical Team Skills

The size, type, and complexity of the project will dictate the skills needed to complete the work. For simple projects, a single resource may wear a number of different hats. During larger implementations, multiple people may be needed to fill a single "role" to ensure you have the knowledge necessary to complete the identified tasks.

These key roles are useful on most projects regardless of size. Again, how many people you need to complete the identified work will define what specific roles people fill and how many people are required in each role.

- *Project manager*: The project manager is the single point of contact for the entire project team. The project manager will be the individual responsible for ensuring that all of the steps and deliverables included in the methodology are carried out. This individual holds primary accountability for the successful delivery of the project and the timely communication of project progress and status to project resources. Additionally, this individual will provide overall direction for the CRM modeling and design, configuration, and customization activities.

- *Analyst(s)*: The analyst on the project will typically own a broad range of tasks. Most elements of application design, configuration/customization, and rollout typically fall to the analyst. Given their functional knowledge of the project, a majority of the test plan development, training plan development, and execution of training classes will be the responsibility of the project analyst.

- *Developer(s)*: The developer will be responsible for building custom code, integration, reports, and data conversion scripts and related deliverables. Should the scope of your project include any architecture or data-focused work, this resource will be the primary point of contact.

- *Tester(s)*: With more complex projects, separate resources may be used to complete the testing of the application and related functionality prior to going live.

- *Other*: Depending on complexity, there are a few other roles that we typically see on CRM projects:

  - CRM architect

  - Dedicated trainer

  - Networking/infrastructure engineers

  - User experience designers

To emphasize, many of these roles, while important, can be filled by the same person for smaller projects.

Internal vs. Vendor Resources

In Chapter 4, we spent time providing information about how to evaluate your resourcing needs relative to using internal vs. vendor resources, specifically, the criteria used to evaluate potential vendors. For the purposes of this chapter, it is imperative to compare resourcing needs with the skills within your organization. Often, when we see organizations try to take on more project tasks than they have the time or skills for, they are adding risk to the project.

Should you need to leverage vendor resources, a vast majority of the items or tasks listed in this chapter will need to be expended to include information from the vendor team. For example, although the vendor may provide you with a status report on their team's tasks and activities, the overall project status will need to be updated to meld internal and vendor resource status.

Vendor resources can definitely assist with the delivery of the implementation, but they will also make the overall project management more complicated. Ultimately, if the project requires both internal and external resources, involving the appropriate vendors will greatly reduce many of the risks on the project.

Change Management

Regardless of how carefully scope is managed during the implementation, the balance between structure and flexibility that we previously discussed, combined with a structured project methodology, will inevitably lead to scope changes. These scope changes can be the result of conscious decision of the project team, or the result of an issue that occurs on the project. When they occur, you can use a number of tools to track these items.

Change Requests

The change request process allows the project team to document the functional and technical updates to the scope of the project. This document should also be used to document and track the impact to hours and budget that the scope change has on the process. You can find more information on the change request process in Chapter 6.

Project Impacts

The project impact document looks very similar to the change request document but is typically presented under less than positive circumstances. Whether an internal issue or one involving a vendor resource, a project impact typically represents a significant risk to the project or something that has consumed a significant amount of unnecessary time or budget and needs to be outlined for the collective project team. Figure 5-8 shows a sample of what a project impact statement might look like.

1.　　Project Impact Overview

Briefly describe the project impact. It should include the steps Madrona took to attempt to prevent the impact.

2.　　Impact of change

It is helpful to describe the process used to identify the additional cost or schedule impacts. Ideally the process should be the same as the process used to estimate original project scope.

Impact on Budget

Role	Hours
Analyst	90
TOTAL	90.0
TOTAL COST	$12,150

Impact on Schedule

Note – this work will be completed within the existing project schedule outlined by the delivery team, or will be completed on an ad hoc basis following go-live.

Risk Impact

Note – this project impact has generated the following project risk.

3.　　Future Mitigation

Describe how to mitigate or account for this same type of impact in the future. There may be impacts that are unavoidable. Under those situations, it should be described how to deal with or recognize the impact at the soonest possible instant.

Figure 5-8. Project impact example

Project Communication

Effectively communicating throughout your project will be a significant factor in its ultimate success. More importantly, how and when you communicate to the collective project team will greatly influence their perception of the project and outcomes. During the planning phase of your project, ensure that you put thought into the various communication medium, communication frequency, and messaging that you will use throughout your project.

Portals as Project Management Tools

Many companies today utilize portal technologies as tools to assist with managing their projects. Much like a status report, a portal can be a tool to accommodate various stakeholder groups and can assist with ensuring appropriate tracking of documents and other information. The following are some specific use cases for portals during your project:

- *Status reporting*: Depending on the size and scope of your project, leveraging a portal as the tool to present your status reports could make viewing and collaboration easier. Within most portals, you have an opportunity to break out summary and detailed information into different sections. This essentially accomplishes the same thing as breaking the status report into distinct sections but saves the project manager from sending an e-mail that may get lost in the recipient's inbox.

- *Document management*: With projects of all sizes, managing, exchanging, and updating documents can be a challenging task. Using a portal technology with document management capabilities can simplify this process. Most of these technologies have the capability to manage check-in/checkout processes, outline changes to a document, and supply version control features to users.

- *General information sharing*: As a project's complexity grows, typically so do the number of resources involved. As the resource list grows to include internal and external (vendor) resources, having a tool to allow collaboration becomes important.

- *Logging:* If your project has any complexity, you are likely to experience some risk during the life of your implementation. A status report can be used to highlight this risk, provide notes or comments on mitigation steps that are being taken, and provide a history of issues encountered and steps taken.

Expectations Setting

Depending on the decision made relative to a phased or big-bang approach, it is important that you focus on setting users' expectations early and often. Many of the issues that arise following a deployment are the result of incorrectly set expectations, not issues with the application. Quite a few of the tools we provide information on in this book can be used in various ways to do this:

- *Kickoff meeting:* The kickoff meeting is a great tool to provide a baseline for the expectations of your organization. Whether provided verbally or documented in a project charter, this meeting may be the first time the larger user community will get information on what is being delivered and when it will be available. Using this meeting as a tool, combined with the ongoing communicated in a status report, will ensure appropriate expectation setting for users.

- *Status report:* As we discussed earlier in this chapter, the messages included in the status report can impact users within your organization. Subtle, or at times not so subtle, messages about scope or delivery timelines, used repeatedly in your status report, will help guide a user's expectations in the long run.

- *Executive communications:* Although executive communication is important when driving excitement or usage of your CRM application, using it as a tool to set users' expectations is also important. A combination of providing updates strategically worded to set expectations and highlighting interesting features of the application will set expectations and drive users' excitement.

In addition to these tools, finding the right individuals in your user community to act as evangelists and work with troubled users can greatly help in ensuring success. Help from a fellow user or peer can be more impactful than that from the "official" CRM implementation team.

Ongoing Project Management

Once you've identified the scope for this phase of your project and, subsequently, the appropriate resources to deliver this scope, you can move into a mode where you are managing to the recognized tasks and schedule. Very much like project planning tools, quite a few options exist when looking at managing high-level information about the status of your project scope, budget, and resources.

Now, we will provide you with examples of some of the normal templates we have historically used during CRM implementations.

Status Management

Once your project begins, you will want to consistently report on the status of the implementation. This status can be used for a number of purposes:

- *Classic project management*: For the good of the project, staying on top of the overall project status and any issues or concerns around project budget, resources, and scope, as well as providing information to your executive steering committee on a regular basis, is very important. Without maintaining and sharing this information, the collective team (end users and the project leadership team) may have mismatched expectations or may not be on the same page relative to important decisions made during the project.

- *Meeting reduction*: With larger projects, the implementation team will frequently have to provide project status to a number of different stakeholder groups. Whether these groups are looking for the same information or information of different depths, you may have to schedule a discussion to provide information. A properly formatted status report will give each of these groups information that should answer many of their status questions at the right level without having to schedule independent meetings.

- *CRM evangelization*: As we discuss throughout the book, driving excitement about CRM and letting those in your organization know about the tool and its capabilities will ultimately impact your project's success. In addition to highlighting more "negative" items like risks or issues, a status report can be used to highlight the positive happenings within a project. You may choose to include highlights of recent wins or upcoming releases that will positively benefit users.

- *Risk mitigation*: Finally, you are likely to experience some risk during the life of your implementation. A status report can be used to highlight this risk, provide notes or comments on mitigation steps that are being taken, and provide a history of issues encountered and steps taken.

The status report example in Figure 5-9 provides a number of items you may choose to include in your customized status report. Depending on the level of complexity of your project, you may include some or all of these sections in the status report you produce. You may also have sections that make sense based on the project management methodology of your organization.

Account:	<Group / Account Name>
Project:	<Project Name>
Document:	Weekly Status Update
Created By:	<Resource Name>
Period Ending:	04/18/2011

Reporting Period:	04/11/2011 – 04/17/2011	Phase:	Initial Design

Project Component	Status	Comment
Scope	◉	<Comment Here>
Schedule	◉	<Comment Here>
Budget	◉	<Comment Here>
Resources	◉	<Comment Here>

Project Milestone	Status
Milestone 1	◉
Milestone 2	◉
Milestone 3	◉
Milestone 4	◉
Milestone 5	◉

Open Issues				
Issue	Date Raised	Assigned To	Status	Resolution Date
Issue 1				
Issue 2				
Issue 3				

Figure 5-9. Summary status report

The first page of the status report provides a high-level status for those interested in seeing a visual representation of the project's status. Readers can scan quick information related to scope, schedule, budget, and resources, and they will be able to evaluate the need for them to become involved with any issues identified using a brief test and a "stoplight" graphic.

For those looking for additional information, you may choose to provide more detailed content, as shown in Figure 5-10.

Account:	\<Group / Account Name>
Project:	\<Project Name>
Document:	Weekly Status Update
Created By:	\<Resource Name>
Period Ending:	04/18/2011

This Period's Accomplishments

- Accomplishment 1
- Accomplishment 2
- Accomplishment 3
- Accomplishment 4
- Accomplishment 5

Next Period's Goals

- Goal 1
- Goal 2
- Goal 3
- Goal 4
- Goal 5

Upcoming Calendar of Events

Date	Description	Attendees

Overall Project Milestones:

Milestone	Original Target	Revised Target	Actual Date	Note

Figure 5-10. Detailed status report

This section of the status report allows you to report on specific tasks worked on during the status reporting period, as well as the items to be focused on during the next reporting period. Providing this information will allow the implementation team to ensure the proper focus on activities from week to week. The upcoming calendar of events section will help those looking at all levels of information to understand what meetings are scheduled for the subsequent reporting period. Finally, the milestone section of the document provides continuous updates on the projected and actual dates for the milestones.

Importance of Process Definition

As we discussed earlier in this chapter, the methodology you choose to implement will have a significant impact on how you approach the design of the application. We will discuss specific design approaches and deliverables later in this chapter. For now, it is imperative to consider the importance of process definition regardless of methodology. One of the most regular, and easiest to address, mistakes made during many CRM projects is to ignore the need to analyze "as is" process and evaluate necessary "to be" process changes that should be included in the implementation phase.

At a very minimum, analyzing the "as is" process will enable the implementation team to ensure that the scope of the project phase includes the necessary functionality to replicate the existing processes in the new application. Ideally, a continued evaluation of "to be" processes will allow the collective team to compare desired processes with the functionality of your chosen CRM application. This may actually help in reducing scope, lowering costs, and reducing risk because some needed, future functionality may be available very simply within the application.

Tracking "Parking Lot" Items

Another item to plan for prior to executing your initial implementation phase is the tracking and managing of scope items deemed important but not part of the current phase of the project. Another common mistake from implementation teams revolves around including additional scope in a project. Once the project begins, the user community can place a significant amount of pressure on the project manager(s) to include new items into the project scope. Although there are absolutely times where this inclusion is merited, the tracking and triaging of these items will enable the project manager and steering committee to make educated decisions about if and how to change scope when requested.

Figure 5-11 shows an example of a simple yet effective spreadsheet used for tracking these items.

Topic	Description	Priority	Sub Priority	Project Area	Category	Owner	Enter Date	Status	Resolution
Topic 1	Provide a complete description.	A	2	Sales	Usability	Adam	7-Mar	Complete	
Topic 2	Provide a complete description.	A	3	Service	Security	Kerry	7-Mar	Investigate	
Topic 3	Provide a complete description.	A	2	Marketing	Reporting	Sarah	7-Mar	Not Started	
Topic 3	Provide a complete description.	A	1		Account	Sarah	7-Mar	Canceled	
Topic 4	Provide a complete description.	A	2		Contact	Sarah	7-Mar		
Topic 5	Provide a complete description.	A	1		Opportunity	Adam	7-Mar		
Topic 6	Provide a complete description.	A	1			Sarah	7-Mar		
Topic 7	Provide a complete description.	B	1			Sarah	7-Mar		
Topic 8	Provide a complete description.	B	2			Mathew	7-Mar		
Topic 9	Provide a complete description.	B	3			Sarah	7-Mar		

Figure 5-11. *Parking lot items tracking example*

1. *Topic and description*: Although extremely basic, the topic and description should be used to capture a high-level, and slightly more detailed, overview of the scope change being reflected. This spreadsheet will be used by the user community at large, so providing an understandable description will head off any questions from users.

2. *Priority and subpriority*: Including both a priority and subpriority allows the project steering committee to get very granular when evaluating new scope requests. Should additional time or budget become available, this detailed ranking of requested scope items will allow a carefully thought out decision to be made around which scope to include.

3. *Owner*: This is yet another simple piece of information to track related to a scope item. That said, it is also very important. The owner of a requested parking lot item will ultimately be responsible for driving additional requirements necessary to make an informed decision about whether to include this scope in the project. Typically, this person is also responsible for initially prioritizing and then presenting this item to the steering committee for review.

4. *Date and resolution*: As we mentioned earlier in this section, the user community at large will likely utilize this spreadsheet to track the progress of their requests. Providing them with updated entry dates and status will allow them to feel comfortable that the request is moving forward.

There are additional data points that could be of value to your project team as well. The most frequently added information is related to dates and ensuring that the user community feels consistently updated about the items that they've requested and placed such high importance on.

The Challenges with Over-customization

Very similar to the issues caused by employing a big-bang approach with the initial phase of your implementation, it is easy for the project team to find themselves in a situation where they over-customize the application in an attempt to meet users' requirements. Over-customization is something that is more likely to happen with larger, multifunctional implementations. As an example, when two sales teams with drastically different interests and sales processes utilize the same implementation, there's the potential to add too many fields, customizations, and automations to the implementation. Ultimately, the addition of too many things into the application has the potential to cause the following:

- *User confusion*: The ability for users to quickly ramp up on the application during training and post-release will make or break the success of your initial implementation. If there are too many fields, or if users receive a significant number of e-mails or tasks generated by the application, they're likely to be confused and abandon the implementation.

- *Unnecessary process impacts*: Very similar to the previous bullet, if the new features of the application require users to jump through process hoops that are unfamiliar to them, they may struggle to adopt the application.

- *Additional support costs*: In situations where over-customization has occurred, users either will struggle with the tool or will require "emergency" changes to allow them to feel more comfortable with the solution developed. In either of these cases, support from an internal or vendor team will be necessary to keep the application moving forward.

Over-customization is an item that can be controlled by the collective implementation team. Leveraging an iterative approach with application reviews to ensure users are comfortable with how the application is being built will prevent a surprise later. Additionally, using classic scope management tools like the status report and project charter, combined with managing parking lot items, will keep the focus of the initial implementation on items that add the most value to the user community.

Budget Management

Depending on how your team functions internally, you may or may not be required to track expense items toward an internal budget. If you are using a vendor, you will definitely want to ensure you're tracking their spending toward your identified budget.

Budget management can be a tricky thing to manage because it is something that's easily gamed by the vendor. How you manage the budget and what tools you use to identify any budget risks is dependent on the kind or size of project you're undertaking.

If you are working on a small initial project, you may only have some spend associated with a kickoff and then some amount of fixed monthly spend moving forward. In situations like this, the important thing to track is spend against budget and the amount of work received on a monthly basis. That will be the key to allowing you to define whether the monthly value meets or exceeds the amount spend, whether internal or external.

Should your team be focused on a larger project for the first phase of your CRM program, the costs are generally quite variable. Effort associated with a larger project can range from a few weeks to a couple of years, and literally everything in between. The tools you use to manage your budget can vary greatly; however, we will provide one example along with thoughts on the value of specific sections. Figure 5-12 shows an example of a tool that could be used to manage budget and track any variance.

Project Billing Summary

Complete
Last Update: 05/06/11

Week Ending		Total Hours	Billable Hours	Comp. Hours	Total Billed	Planned Billing	Eff. Rate	Remaining Budget
Approved Project Budget								$ 175,000
Complete	04/22/11	120.00	120.00	0.00	$ 19,600.00	$ -	$ 163.33	$ 155,400
Complete	04/29/11	95.00	95.00	0.00	$ 15,350.00	$ -	$ 161.58	$ 140,050
In Progress	05/06/11	95.00	95.00	0.00	$ -	$ 15,350.00	--	$ 140,050
Planned	05/13/11	95.00	95.00	0.00	$ -	$ 15,350.00	--	$ 140,050
Planned	05/20/11	95.00	95.00	0.00	$ -	$ 15,350.00	--	$ 140,050
Planned	05/27/11	59.00	59.00	0.00	$ -	$ 9,230.00	--	$ 140,050
Planned	06/03/11	55.00	55.00	0.00	$ -	$ 8,550.00	--	$ 140,050
Planned	06/10/11	55.00	55.00	0.00	$ -	$ 8,550.00	--	$ 140,050
Planned	06/17/11	55.00	55.00	0.00	$ -	$ 8,550.00	--	$ 140,050
Planned	06/24/11	55.00	55.00	0.00	$ -	$ 8,550.00	--	$ 140,050
Planned	07/01/11	55.00	55.00	0.00	$ -	$ 8,550.00	--	$ 140,050
Planned	07/08/11	55.00	55.00	0.00	$ -	$ 8,550.00	--	$ 140,050
Planned	07/15/11	55.00	55.00	0.00	$ -	$ 8,550.00	--	$ 140,050
Planned	07/22/11	55.00	55.00	0.00	$ -	$ 8,550.00	--	$ 140,050
Planned	07/28/11	55.00	55.00	0.00	$ -	$ 8,550.00	--	$ 140,050
Planned	08/05/11	0.00	0.00	0.00	$ -	$ -	No Billable Time	$ 140,050
Planned	08/12/11	0.00	0.00	0.00	$ -	$ -	No Billable Time	$ 140,050
Planned	08/19/11	0.00	0.00	0.00	$ -	$ -	No Billable Time	$ 140,050
Planned	08/26/11	0.00	0.00	0.00	$ -	$ -	No Billable Time	$ 140,050
Planned	09/02/11	0.00	0.00	0.00	$ -	$ -	No Billable Time	$ 140,050
Planned	09/09/11	0.00	0.00	0.00	$ -	$ -	No Billable Time	$ 140,050
Planned	09/16/11	0.00	0.00	0.00	$ -	$ -	No Billable Time	$ 140,050
Planned	09/23/11	0.00	0.00	0.00	$ -	$ -	No Billable Time	$ 140,050
Totals		1,054.00	1,054.00	0.00	$ 34,950.00	$ 132,230.00		$ 140,050

Estimated Fees

Original Estimate	$175,000.00
Existing Fees	$0.00
Project Impact	$0.00
Change Requests	$ -
Complimentary Fees	$0.00
Total Approved Estimate	$175,000.00
Billed To-Date	$34,950
% Over/Under Estimate	4.47% Under Estimate
Invoiced-To-Date	$ 87,000.00
% Fees Invoiced	49.71%

Invoicing Summary

Amount	Date	Remaining
$ 15,000.00	4/22/2011	$160,000.00
$ 22,000.00	4/29/2011	$138,000.00
$ 50,000.00	5/5/2011	$88,000.00
		$88,000.00
		$88,000.00

Hours Summary

Total Budgeted	1,166.67
Total Remaining	112.67

Figure 5-12. Budget tracking example

1. *Total spend to budget tracking:* This piece of the tool provides you with the ability to look at the total allotted budget and see how much has been spent. Depending on the status of the project, you may have to make some educated decisions about how much should be available, but ultimately, the data here will assist you with making that determination.

2. *Remaining budget:* At any point in the project, you will have the availability to look at a single number and understand how much budget is remaining.

3. *Weekly budget expenditures:* Viewing weekly budget hours and spend is a very important piece to the budget management puzzle. First, this visibility allows you to overlay weekly spend with your project plan to ensure the two match. Second, this

allows you to make the more important budget determination for big projects, such as how much budget remains and whether it is appropriately spread across the remainder of the project.

4. *Invoice status*: Project managers and vendor resources are often tasked with providing updates to invoicing status in addition to the classic budget. Using this template, you can provide the steering committee with dates and amounts of any invoices submitted by the vendor.

5. *Project impacts and change request tracking*: Simple automation in this template can give you the ability to track project impacts and change requests in the same place as the original budget. By adding them to this spreadsheet, the overall budget number will increase, allowing the project management team to utilize the total budget number when evaluating budget status.

6. *Overall budget status*: By incorporating all of the items into the budget spreadsheet, you will be able to instantly tell what percent over or under budget the project is.

The larger the project, the more likely the risk that the budget will be spent inappropriately. In larger projects, there is a risk that the team will spend 80 percent of the budget to deliver 10 percent of the functionality. Once this happens, the implementation team is in a difficult position because they've made promises to the user community, but the costs continue to be significantly more than previously expected.

Ultimately, the most important thing for the project management team to understand is the status of the budget at any point in time. Whether that status relates to total spend, upcoming spend, or simply how many hours will be used during a current week, finding a mechanism to provide this information is key.

Issue Management

Although we may begin to sound repetitive, being prepared to manage issues is yet another important facet of planning the project. Much like parking lot items and status reports, having issues be transparent to users will go a long way toward allowing them to trust the implementation team. In addition to this potential value, managing issues is about accountability and risk.

To successfully manage issues throughout the life of a project, having a mechanism to track them, however simple, is important. This tool will also allow the core project team to manage the ownership of those issues to ensure the proper follow-up and triage by folks on the project team. Figure 5-13 shows one example of a simple yet effective template you can use to track issues.

e	Current Action	Description / Summary	Affects	Assigned To	Last Action	Resolution
Issue 1	Backburner	Provide a complete description to the issue	Sales	Ron	19-Apr	Provide a summary of the resolution to the issue.
Issue 2	Closed		Service	Ron	19-Apr	
Issue 3	Vendor Team investigating		Marketing	Sarah	14-Apr	
Issue 4	Internal Team investigating		All	Mathew	21-Apr	
Issue 5	Submitted as bug to Support		Administration	Ron	19-Apr	
Issue 6	To be discussed with CRM Team			Ron	19-Apr	

Figure 5-13. Issue management tracking example

Resource/Vendor Management

Regardless of the size of your project, you will have resources of some sort to manage. Like many of the activities associated with planning and managing the project, setting the appropriate expectations up front will enable you to be more successful in the long run.

If your focus is on internal resources, one mistake we frequently see is not allowing enough time for internal resources to complete tasks. Unless your organization is fortunate enough to have individuals who have worked on CRM projects in the past, many tasks will take longer than expected. Additionally, depending on the politics of your organization, you may need to spend additional time communicating resource status with the project steering committee. Regardless of the situation, your project management tools—specifically, the resourcing components of the project plan and the status report—can help you manage resource expectations internally.

If you are dealing with a project involving vendors, the situation becomes more complicated. All of the same techniques used to manage internal resources can also be used to manage vendors. A vendor organization will typically provide some amount of project management time on top of their implementation time. Like internal resources, vendor resources will be a component of the project plan, and their efforts should be part of any status updates.

Most vendors we have had the opportunity to work with are extremely reputable and place a focus on doing what is in the best interest of their clients. Unfortunately, there are some vendors whose reputation is less than stellar. For those, here are some issues you might want consider as you work through an implementation process involving vendors.

- *Bait and switch*: In some situations during the sales cycle, vendors will present a person as the resource for a project and then will switch the resource before the project begins. Although consulting organizations rarely commit to specific resources before the contract is executed, the resources eventually assigned to your project should be consistent in skills and experience with the promises made during the sales process.

- *Spend vs. budget*: As we outlined during the budget management section of this chapter, careful management of budget and hours will ensure that the budget consistently aligns with the needed effort. Completing a significant percent of the project but not having budget to finish the implementation will put the whole team at a significant disadvantage.

- *The "partner model"*: As a group implementing CRM, there will be enough costs without adding unneeded overhead. Some consulting organizations implement a partner model where a senior-level resource will bill time on projects without providing the requisite value. Make sure that those involved with the engagement, senior or junior, are providing value to the implementation.

- *Knowledge transfer*: It is very easy for vendors to focus on the implementation without providing the information needed to the internal project team. Confirm that your vendor has included enough time to properly support the deployment of the tool and transfer information including code, documents, and process knowledge to the internal team.

- *Tools vs. process:* Consultants bring varying approaches to the specific CRM tool and the associated implementation. At times, it is easy for consultants to focus on the tool and mold an organization's processes to fit the available functionality. You should make sure that the vendor is prepared to mold the tool to meet your organization's process needs instead of changing your processes to fit within the tool.

- *Consulting training:* Every consultant will have a first project, but to ensure ultimate success for your organization, it is important that you understand the background of the team the vendor brings to bear. If a more junior resource is being put on the project, ensure they have the appropriate backing of the vendor organization and ask for a discounted rate to account for the resource's inevitable ramp-up period.

These examples are just some of the pitfalls you may experience when working with a vendor team. To reiterate, with most vendors, you may not encounter any of these issues, but going into the project situation aware of the potential hazards will prevent issues in the long run.

Typical Vendor Contracts

The type and format of contracts utilized by vendors vary greatly; however, there are two high-level types of documents that it may make sense to have between your organization and any vendors involved in the project.

The first document is typically called a *professional services agreement* (PSA) or *master services agreement* (MSA). The classic purpose for this document is to outline the terms and conditions governing the relationship between the two organizations. This document will be an umbrella document under which any project work is defined and completed.

The second normal document is often called a statement of work (SOW). This document is specific to a project and usually covers a project's scope, assumptions, deliverables, and individual project costs.

Figure 5-14 shows a sample table of contents from a PSA outlining some of the items you should expect to see, and some comments, when presented with this document from your vendor.

CONTENTS

1 SERVICES, MASTER AGREEMENT 3
- 1.1 Services 3
- 1.2 Master Agreement 3

2 FEES, INVOICES AND PAYMENT 4
- 2.1 Fees 4
- 2.2 Invoices and Payment 4

3 WORK SCHEDULES; PERSONNEL 4

4 CONFIDENTIAL INFORMATION 4
- 4.1 Restricted Use and Disclosure 5

5 WARRANTIES OF MADRONA SOLUTIONS 5
- 5.1 Limited Warranty 5
- 5.2 Disclaimer 6

6 RIGHTS IN DATA 6

7 LIMITATION OF LIABILITY 6

8 TERM AND TERMINATION 6
- 8.1 Stated Term 6
- 8.2 Earlier Termination by Client 7
- 8.3 Earlier Termination By vENDOR When No SOW Outstanding 7
- 8.4 Termination by Either Party for Cause 7
- 8.5 Termination of Statement of Work 7

9 FREEDOM OF ACTION/OTHER CONSULTANTS 7

10 EMPLOYEE SOLICITATION 8

11 NOTICES 8

12 INDEPENDENT CONTRACTOR 8

13 WORK STOPPAGE 8
- 13.1 Forced Work Stoppage 8
- 13.2 Unforced Work Stoppage 9

14 COMPENSATION OF Madrona Solutions EMPLOYEES 9

15 ASSIGNMENT 9

16 MISCELLANEOUS 9
- 16.1 Waiver 9
- 16.2 Referrals 9
- 16.3 Attorney Fees 9
- 16.4 Modifications 10
- 16.5 Resolution of Disputes 10

17 GOVERNING LAW 10

2 | PROFESSIONAL SERVICES AGREEMENT | CONFIDENTIAL

Figure 5-14. *PSA table of contents*

Here are some key items to focus on:

1. *Invoicing structure*: A standard PSA will outline the invoicing terms between you and the vendor. These terms include both invoicing frequency and the standard payment terms you will be expected to follow when paying the vendor invoices. As a starting point, most vendors invoice either every two weeks or monthly and typically request Net 30 payment terms.

2. *Confidential information*: Virtually every PSA will contain a clause on confidential information. Depending on how friendly your vendor's PSA is, this clause may be bidirectional or may be focused solely on protecting the vendor's confidential documents and information. Obviously, from your organization's perspective, this clause also needs to include protections for your information, documents, and processes uncovered during the project.

3. *Rights in data:* Overall, the rights in data section of the document will discuss who owns the deliverables of any project work performed by the vendor. Although this seems pretty straightforward, this section can become complicated with CRM projects. Because you are paying for the project, it is reasonable for you to assume that you will own any intellectual property developed during the project. The challenge arises when you discuss ownership of configurations. As you might imagine, if you add a field called "Account Name" to your CRM application, a vendor cannot give you exclusive ownership of this customization because many of their future clients will request the same form. For that reason, the rights in data section often includes some joint ownership of customizations, and you should expect this when reviewing the PSA.

4. *Employee solicitation*: Much like the confidential information section, this section of the PSA may be bidirectional or may protect the vendor only from you hiring their resources. Ultimately, you may both want this protection during the project to ensure resources are continuously focused on the tasks at hand.

5. *Resolution and disputes*: This section of the PSA handles any issues should they arise between you and the vendor. This section will discuss where any disputes will be resolved and, if appropriate, whether arbitration is a component of this

agreement. Based on our experience, including an arbitration clause is a good idea on the off-chance something comes up, because it will allow you to avoid legal action as long as possible.

One overall item for you to consider when reviewing the PSA is how bidirectional the clauses in the document are. A significant amount of the document can and should be bi-directional. As an example, if the vendor asks you to avoid hiring their resources, it's only fair for you to expect the same.

Figure 5-15 shows the table of contents from a typical SOW.

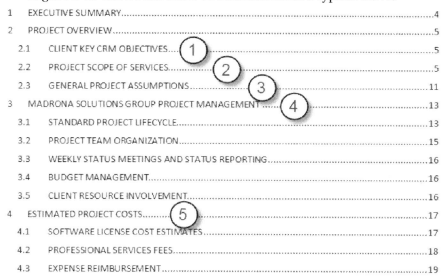

Figure 5-15. *Statement of work table of contents*

6. *Key objectives*: Although this section of most SOWs is short, it is an opportunity for the vendor to articulate their understanding of the goals of this project. The items may be at a summary level, but if significant items are missing from the objectives list, consider bringing them up with your vendor.

7. *Project scope of services*: The scope section of the document is the most important section of the SOW. This section will outline the specific scope, customizations, code, integrations, and so on, that will be delivered as part of the project. The scope section will provide the items to be delivered, specific deliverables associated with those scope items, and any assumptions made by the vendor to box the scope item to the appropriate level.

8. *General assumptions:* This section differs from the assumptions identified in the scope section because it handles some higher-level assumptions about the project. Some items such as reporting, workflow, training, and deployment functions are able to be handled with a bucket of time (as opposed to a specific scope item) and may have associated general assumptions.

9. *Vendor project management:* In our experience, some vendors provide detailed information about their project management methodology and delivery model in the SOW, but others do not. If you have the option to ask the vendor to include this information, it will give you visibility into their methodology early in the process.

10. *Estimated project costs:* The costs section of the SOW will be key to deciding whether to move forward with a solution. This section will include three primary components:

    a. *Software:* Regardless of the type of application chosen (hosted or on premise), some software costs will exist. Ensure that your vendor provides costs associated with the different models. This is also the section where any third-party software costs should be provided.

    b. *Services:* The professional services costs associated with the scope items outlined in the SOW will be outlined here. Those costs should include implementation costs, post-deployment support costs, and the cost of any project management provided by the vendor.

    c. *Travel:* Although not all projects will include travel, ensuring that the vendor has identified any expected costs, including estimates for a hotel, rental car, airfare/transportation, and/or per diem, will prevent any confusion down the road. You may also want to ensure that the vendor conforms to your travel policies, including getting travel approved in advance or using a preferred hotel.

As we mentioned earlier in this section, contracts vary greatly from vendor to vendor. Ensuring that they continue most or all of the items we've outlined will allow you to cover as many bases as possible prior to beginning the implementation.

Executive Support

Once you have completed all the planning tasks and document generation needed to be prepared for your project, it is necessary for you to gather all the executive support needed to begin. Throughout this book, we discuss the value of having an executive team that supports your overall CRM program. At this point, that focus should be on the specific project at hand.

Executive support at this point in the implementation can come from two primary sources: a single, high-level executive and the project steering committee. Whether focused on simply kicking off the project or on gaining alignment with the overall project team, the project charter document can be a tool to ensure the team is moving in the same, and correct, direction.

The project charter should be developed by members of the core project team. A number of the key charter items, such as risks, project schedule, and project dependencies, require input from various stakeholders and may not be known solely by the project manager. Looping in, and getting buy-off, from those involved in any risks or scheduling dependencies will ensure the project manager has the ability to effectively manage those issues should they arise during the project. After you have worked with the team to develop the charter, you should plan to roll it out to the whole team and solicit feedback. Figure 5-16 is an example of a project charter table of contents.

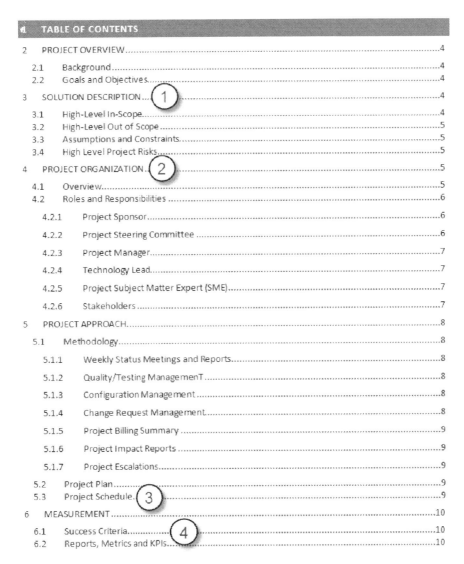

Figure 5-16. Project charter table of contents

Some keys to this document include the following:

1.   *Solution description*: Because many of those involved in the project will not have been in discussions with the project sponsor (and vendor, if appropriate) about project scope, outlining what is in scope and, just as importantly, what is out of

scope will give the project team an opportunity to provide comments. Should anyone on the project team disagree with someone that's in or out of scope, a follow-up discussion to discuss is appropriate.

2. *Project organization*: Although the project organization section seems pretty straightforward, correctly identifying up front which people will fill specific roles will prevent confusion from the larger project team and users later. Members of the core project team, including SMEs, the project manager, and the technology lead, and the steering committee will be expected to make decisions during the project, so the project charter can assist with ensuring people in those roles understand their responsibilities.

3. *Project schedule*: An overview of the key milestones for the project will allow the overall project team to make certain that conflicts do not exist that could jeopardize the project schedule. If these conflicts do exist, a follow-up discussion can occur to attempt to mitigate any risk associated with them or identify necessary changes to the project schedule.

4. *Success criteria*: The final and most important piece, to the project charter is identifying project success criteria. Allowing the project team to assist with the definition of these items will guarantee that they are invested in the success of the project. Because of the often nebulous nature of the value provided by CRM engagements, clearly documenting the success criteria will enable you to articulate the success of the project following deployment and will greatly aid in getting funding or resources for future phases.

Like most documents highlighted throughout this book, the project charter your organization uses may differ from the previous one. Some companies utilize a single-page summary document based on PowerPoint, others use something more complex, but including the four key items identified will garner alignment among the project team members.

Summary

Throughout this chapter, we discussed items you should focus on as you plan for and manage your initial deployment. Depending on the size and complexity of your engagement, some of these items may be overkill, but looking for an opportunity to use a scaled-down version of the documents will ensure you do not miss anything during the project.

We initially focused on the planning or approach you're going to take with your project. Making sure the schedule meets the needs of your stakeholders, evaluating the big bang vs. phased approach, and securing a team of resources to deliver the work will act as a foundation for the rest of the project-planning activities. We next covered the ongoing project management activities needed to keep the project running smoothly. Lastly, and probably most importantly, we discussed building and communicating support from your executive team to keep the project moving in the proper direction. Whether driving excitement, ensuring resource commitments, or addressing issues, the support and engagement from your executive team will be felt across the entire project.

In the next chapter, we will discuss the actual execution of your project. We will cover topics such as design, development, testing, and training, as well as other items.

CHAPTER 6

Executing the Initial CRM Implementation

In the previous chapter, we have provided you with the steps necessary to plan the initial project of your CRM program. Not all of the outlined tools and methods are useful in all situations; ultimately, you will find the items that make sense for you to use based on your organization and the complexity of your planned implementation.

In this chapter, we will focus on executing the initial implementation of your CRM program. We will focus on the various stages of the implementation and will provide information on the templates and processes you should use to execute the implementation. Like the previous chapter, many of the items we will review should be tailored to meet the needs of your organization and project.

The Design Stage

In the previous chapter, we reviewed the various design approaches and methodologies that could be used during your implementation. While all can be successful, we recommend an iterative approach to the design phase.

"As Is" Process Definition

One commonly overlooked step in the design phase of most implementations is the documentation and analysis of an organization's current, or "as is," processes. Documenting and ensuring consensus on process items will allow you to receive two benefits:

- *Application alignment*: An item that we will discuss later in the chapter is the alignment of your application with your organization's business processes. One of the largest CRM implementation gotchas is allowing the technology to drive usage scenarios and business process. Defining your process up front will enable you to ensure that your implementation team, including vendors, are working diligently toward making the application meet your business processes and not the technology's process.

- *Process updates*: Analyzing your processes up front will enable your team to review those processes and determine whether they are appropriate for the company moving forward. Spending time to review how each process might change or be made better will again allow you to make sure the application will meet those needs.

The process document shown in Figure 6-1 is an example of a simple process flow. It combines a normal box-to-box process flow with what is often called a *swim-lane* process flow. The swim lanes allow you to break up the process flow by the person or department involved, enabling them to effectively comment on the accuracy of the process flow and allowing you to see the impacts that an application might have on a specific role.

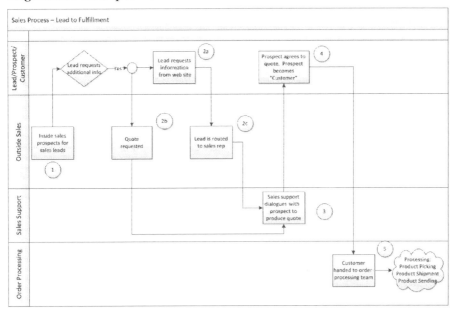

Figure 6-1. *"As is" process flow diagram*

In the process diagram shown in Figure 6-1, you'll note that there are four roles, or *personas*, represented. Depending on how the diagram is structured and what technology you use to build the diagrams, you may also have the ability to link a high-level process flow to more detailed process flows. Additionally, you may choose to highlight specific pieces of the diagram and provide additional detail or content about a box or activity. To do this, you can utilize numbered bubbles like in Figure 6-1 and add comments in a separate but related document.

As you work through the "as is" process analysis, consider identifying not just the steps or actions that occur but also the outputs of the process. If, at any point, a report or document is produced, use the analysis process as an opportunity to spend time evaluating the current outputs and how those items will change with a new CRM system.

"To Be" Process Definition

Once you have assessed the "as is" process, it becomes important for you to evaluate that process with a critical eye toward making improvements in the process and identifying opportunities for the application to automate critical functions, to improve business auditing, or to streamline communications. These conversations are often painful for users because many are used to operating a certain way, or according to a certain process. While it may take time, working through changes in the process now will ultimately make your implementation more successful.

The "as is" process flow can be used as a starting point for any defined "to be" processes. Highlighting any changes will make comparing the two easier in the future. Finally, you should consider using some symbol to highlight any defined automation points when developing the new process.

Figure 6-2 shows the "as is" process flow with some small changes identified, creating a "to be" process flow.

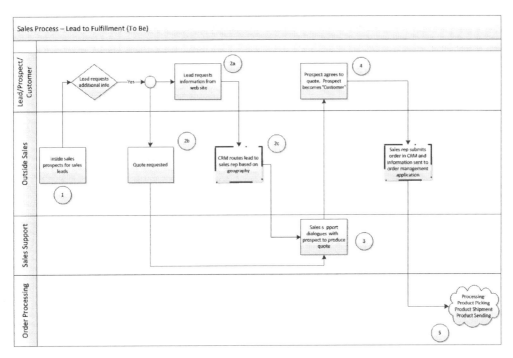

Figure 6-2. *"To be" process flow diagram*

While the changes are small, you will notice a few differences in this process flow, highlighted by the two boxes with a thicker border. Both of these changes represent a change in process as well as an automation that can be facilitated by the application.

Rules and Escalations

Once you have defined the processes, both "as is" and "to be," you should clearly document the automations you have identified as part of the process analysis. At this point, this documentation can be relatively high level but should capture the important characteristics of each piece of automation.

Figure 6-3 provides a simple template for tracking business rules and automations.

1   Business Rule Tracking

1.1   Account Entity

ID	Rule Name	Rule Description	Triggers	Results	Code Type	Notes
1	Account Follow Up	This rule will automate the follow up with an account that makes a purchase from the organization. The follow up will occur 30 days after the initial order is placed with the company. This rule will send an email to the customer with text thanking them for their purchase and offering support for any issues that may arise. Specific text is: "Thank you…"	Order placement will trigger the rule to begin. Then a wait period of 30 days will exist.	An email is sent to the customer per the rule description.	Standard Workflow	
…	…	…	…	…	…	…

1.2   Opportunity Entity

ID	Rule Name	Rule Description	Triggers	Results	Code Type	Notes
1						
…	…	…	…	…	…	…

Figure 6-3. Business rule tracking template

Most of the columns in the template are self-explanatory. Depending on the CRM application you choose, different types of code or CRM functionality will be used to implement a specific piece of automation.

Use Case Definition

Many organizations choose to center the design process around a set of *use cases*. Use cases describe, in a step-by-step manner, the interactions between a user and an application to accomplish some task. Defining use cases is an opportunity for your team to reach consensus on the user scenarios and processes that the application needs to address. For even simple implementations, a number of use cases will be needed to outline the user's tasks and processes. For larger, new application implementations, dozens of use cases may be needed. Use cases, and what they outline, should not be confused with an application feature, because they will differ greatly. Use case definition will assist in two primary ways:

- *Process alignment*: The development and refinement of use cases provide a convenient structure to have detailed process discussions and ensure that all parties are on the same page with respect to the steps, actors, and rationale for the process. Securing this alignment early in the design process makes subsequent work smoother and helps prevent unwelcome surprises late in the design process when process disparities can sometimes surface.

- *Complete testing:* Developing use cases during the design phase will help ensure that complete testing is done during the testing phase of the deployment. Far too often, end-to-end system tests are completed based on what was built, not on the approved design (and intended to be built). This is an important distinction. Designing use cases will provide a baseline set of information for the testing plans developed during a later phase of the engagement.

Figure 6-4 shows an example of a template that can be used to document your use cases.

Use Cases

Use Case #1: New Customer Creation

Summary:

Business Need	
Description	
Author	
Issues / Questions	
Assumptions	
Pre-Conditions	
Successful End Conditions	
Failure End Conditions	
Notes	

Process Flow Diagram:

Figure 6-4 . Use case example

Here is a quick overview of the information included in each section of the use case document:

- *Business need:* Provide a high-level overview or title of the business process being addressed by the use case.

- *Description*: Utilize the description field to capture a more detailed explanation of the business process that the specific user case addresses. If you can provide a before and after view of the use case, you may be able to use this information to evaluate the ultimate success of your engagement.

- *Author*: The author is the person writing the use case.

- *Issues/questions*: Often, when writing a user case, you may identify issues that will impact how the system is implemented to address the use case. Additionally, if you are able to identify and summarize any questions for the project team as they review this use case, you can track them here.

- *Assumptions*: If you make any assumptions about the business process being addressed or users (often referred to as *actors* in use cases) involved, this is the place to document that information. Carefully documenting assumptions is one key to success with use cases. Often, use cases are turned into user testing plans, so documenting assumptions about what leads to a use case, or the process steps that occur as part of a use case, will allow easier generation of the test plan and more effective testing.

- *Preconditions*: Preconditions allow you to define the things that must occur before the process identified in the user case is "allowed" to happen, such as an approval of some kind.

- *Triggers*: Use the triggers section to document the user or process actions that kick off the steps identified in the use case. Using the example of a student attempting to register for college classes, the start of a semester, the opening of a new class, and so on, are all triggers for needing to complete the registration process.

- *Successful end conditions*: This section of the template can be used to document the criteria that indicate a successful completion of the use case. For example, using the same student registration example, a successful end condition would be that the student was allowed to successfully register using whatever application we've designed.

- *Failed end conditions*: This section of the template can be used to document the criteria that indicate a failed end to the use case. For example, if the previously mentioned student isn't allowed, or isn't able to utilize the application to register for class, this could be documented as a failed end condition.

- *Notes*: The notes section of the use case document can be used to track any other information that doesn't fit cleanly into one of the previously identified document sections.

In addition to the template provided in Figure 6-4, use cases often include a flow of information as well as mock-ups or wireframes of how the application will address the needs of the specific user case. Figure 6-5 shows an example of how this information flow and mock-up might be shown for a reporting use case.

Before	Keeping track of lead, opportunity and pipeline data is useless unless you can easily access and analyze it. Through its dynamic link to real-time CRM data, the CRM application makes quick work of accurately viewing sales data and creating easy-to-understand charts. This scenario demonstrates the ease of creating an Excel pivot table and chart that paints a clear picture of the sales pipeline.		
1	Without ever leaving Outlook, I'm now running a sophisticated report that's linked to real-time data in CRM. And it took only a few clicks. This is where, for me as a sales manager and analyst, the power of the CRM application comes in.	a.	In the Pivot Table Field List, select "Est. Revenue", "Potential Customer" and "Rating."	
2	Turning rows of data into an easily understood graph is a few clicks away. Under Pivot Table Options, I select Pivot Chart. A range of chart types is displayed. I think a column chart will be easiest to understand, so I select that.	a.	Click Options, Pivot Chart.	
3	The chart has pulled all of the information about my open opportunities, and whether they're hot, warm or cold. It also displays and potential value of each.			

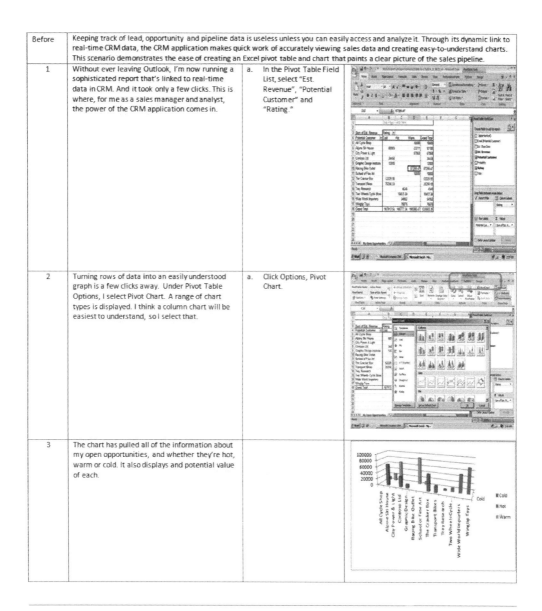

Figure 6-5. Detailed use case example

The example shown in Figure 6-5 can also be used as the basis for a user acceptance test plan**Error! Bookmark not defined.**. Providing clear steps, where those steps occur, and a visible example of how users might interact with the application will allow them to completely test the application.

Functional Specification Development

The final piece of the design puzzle, which brings together all of the elements that we have introduced so far, is the functional specification document. This document is intended to describe the anticipated or expected business behavior of the application you implement. You will notice that many of the items represented in Figure 6-6 document requirements or assumptions from process or design discussions that have occurred as part of the project.

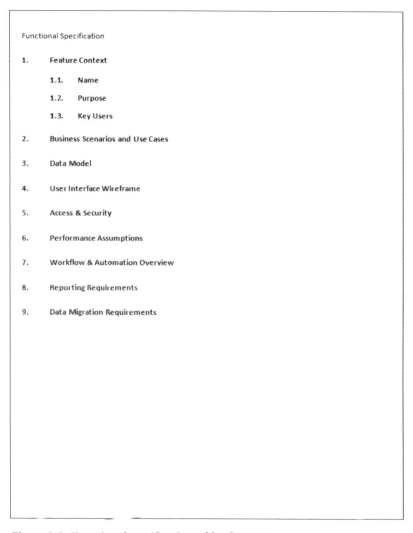

Figure 6-6 . Functional specification table of contents

You will notice that most of the items in Figure 6-6 have been reviewed or discussed at various points during the design phase. The functional specification document can act as the mechanism to consolidate all of the individual process and workflow requirements.

Once your project team has approved the functional specification, the other document that can be produced at this point in the design process is a technical specification document. The technical specification is a document created by the development team to outline the design, development, and testing plan for application components that cannot be built using the standard configuration or workflow tools available in your CRM application. We will provide additional information on the technical specification document in the "Custom Development" section of this chapter.

Before wrapping up the design phase of your project, remember to at least consider the following common design pitfalls:

- *Delayed report design*: Because many organizations focus so heavily on feature and form design initially, the identification and design of any reporting requirements are often overlooked. By designing reports up front, or, at the very least, in parallel with the rest of the features and forms, will ensure that the necessary outputs from the application are considered in the overall design.

- *Data migration errors*: Don't save the design of the data migration until the end of the design phase or the beginning of the build phase. Like reports, make certain you are working on the data migration throughout the design phase. The data being moved from your previous applications will have some limitations around how and to where it is transferred in your new CRM application. Knowing these limitations and addressing them through the design of CRM will make the whole data migration process go much more smoothly.

- *Technology vs. process*: We mentioned this pitfall earlier in this chapter, and we will discuss it in more detail later, but guaranteeing your team has a commitment to sticking to your business process and, more importantly, pushing your chosen CRM application to meet those process requirements will be one of the most important keys to the success of your implementation.

Custom Development

There are likely to be situations where the standard capabilities of your chosen CRM application cannot adequately support your process, or where additional capabilities could have a dramatic impact on your team's productivity. All of the major CRM application vendors have anticipated this and have, to varying degrees, designed their applications to allow them to be augmented with new features by their partners and customers. Because custom features are designed by you, for your unique needs and situation, they can be tremendously valuable. However, there are a number of important considerations before embarking on a custom development effort as part of a CRM project:

- Cost: Custom development involves programming, often from scratch, new features or capabilities for your CRM application. This can be expensive, and the total development costs can be difficult to estimate precisely until all of the design work for the custom components is complete. This can result in cost overruns.

- Upgrade path: Adding custom code to your CRM application can make upgrading from one version to the next more difficult, and the code will require testing and potentially rework with each new release of the CRM application.

- Your own IT resources: Do you have the internal resources with the skills and bandwidth to build, or at least to maintain and periodically enhance, a custom component? If not, how strong is your relationship with your CRM consulting partner? Will there likely be good future continuity with them as your development partner? Are you comfortable with the cost impact of outsourcing this?

- CRM vendor road map: Are you planning to build a feature that is on your CRM application vendor's road map? If so, can it wait?

- ISV landscape: Can this capability be adequately met by an ISV add-on for your CRM application? It is almost always better to purchase an off-the-shelf product than develop custom components, all capabilities being equal.

Our intent is not to dissuade you from pursuing custom development; indeed, some of the most valuable and transformative CRM programs we have seen have included custom-developed components to address directly customer-specific processes and challenges. But the value of these components must be considered thoughtfully, and they must be managed carefully, because they can pose a risk to your project budget and schedule.

Managing Custom Development As Part of Your CRM Project

If you elect to include the development of custom components as part of your CRM project, understand that it is a fundamentally different activity than the design and configuration process associated with the standard application functionality. If that process is analogous to choosing the options and color for your new car, custom development is closer to designing the car from scratch. This difference suggests several guidelines to managing the custom development part of your project:

- Be rigorous about documentation. Create a detailed functional specification as an output of your design process, and keep it up-to-date as the design changes.

- Plan several interim development milestones to assess prototypes, especially for complex components. This allows you an opportunity to get a tangible sense of development progress and to make course corrections as needed.

- Avoid feature creep. Expanding the feature set will impact budget and schedule by a factor larger than just the additional development cost for the new feature. There will always be the opportunity for another release, so don't try to do everything at once; rather, capture desired but out-of-scope features in such a way that they can be reviewed and prioritized for future development.

- Manage offshore development teams carefully. There is a growing trend in the marketplace to outsource custom development work to geographies where these services can be performed at lower cost. This can be a successful model but requires more effort on your part to ensure it is successful. Make sure you select your development partner carefully. Find one with significant experience with your chosen CRM application. Plan to make your documentation more detailed than typical. Without face-to-face interaction, there are fewer opportunities to clarify things, and it can be more difficult to do so via phone/e-mail. Plan for a regular touch point with the development partner on progress. Monitor their workload to make sure you are using their time efficiently.

Technical Specification Documentation

The functional specification defines *what* is to be built. It focuses on outcomes and use cases, and it describes what the application should do, for whom, and at what stage of what process. The technical specification is focused on *how*: what must be built to deliver the capabilities described by the functional spec. While the functional spec is an analyst-driven document, with input from the development team, the technical spec is a developer-driven document, with input from the analyst/design team. There are a number of styles and variations of technical specifications, but most will address the topics in Figure 6-7.

Technical Specification

1.   Introduction

2.   System Architecture

3.   Sequence Diagrams

4.   Presentation Tier Objects

5.   Middle Tier Objects

6.   Database Objects

7.   Screen Specifications

8.   Data Schema

9.   Special Considerations

10.   Volume Considerations

     10.1.   Testing Considerations

     10.2.   Production Support Considerations

     10.3.   Setup and Deployment Considerations

     10.4.   Performance Considerations

11.   Review & Sign-Off

Figure 6-7. Technical specification table of contents

Integration

Application integration is a common component of CRM projects and can add tremendously to the value and impact of your CRM application. We'll define integration for the purposes of this book as programmatically linking business applications together; so, for example, data from one application is visible within the other, or an action in one application can trigger a different action in another. Common rationales for integration include providing a more complete customer picture and automating business processes. Let's examine each in greater detail.

Provide a More Complete Customer Picture

A potential benefit often ascribed to CRM programs is to achieve a "360-degree view" of your customer: one place and one application where an employee can browse all of the organization's interactions with a customer, across all departments. Designed, as it is, with the customer at the center, CRM applications are a natural fit to play this role, but without application integration, this vision cannot be realized. Your organization will continue to need specialized business applications to manage certain types of customer information. Your accounting application, for example, will manage invoices and payments. Integration can make this information available within the CRM application, in the context of the customer, so that alongside native CRM data like sales opportunities, service tickets, and e-mail communications, your CRM users can also view credit status, invoices, and payments from the accounting application. Other applications can be integrated in the same way so that eventually CRM becomes a central place where users can get a full picture of the customer. This allows customer-facing employees to present a single face to the customer and deliver more meaningful and satisfying interactions.

Automate Business Processes

Many customer business processes cross application boundaries. For example, the process of onboarding a new customer begins in the CRM application with a won sales opportunity or order but soon crosses into accounting, where a new customer record must be set up, order fulfillment initiated, and perhaps an invoice prepared. For services organizations, the sold project and customer may need to get created in an enterprise project management application.

Without application integration, the points where these processes cross an application boundary can be associated with delays, redundant, error-prone data entry, and incomplete information. Information from one application must be manually rekeyed into another. An action or event in one department must be communicated to others, via e-mail, phone, or a meeting.

Application integration allows these interactions between applications to occur programmatically, triggered by application events and occurring without user intervention. When a company's status changes from "prospect" to "customer" in the CRM application, the customer information is automatically passed to accounting, and a corresponding customer record is created. Perhaps the accounting team receives an automated e-mail to alert them of this event. If a services-type sales opportunity is won, that event in CRM can trigger the creation of a customer and project record in the enterprise project management application so that the delivery team can get to work planning for service delivery.

In another form of integration to automate business process, an element of another application's user interface is embedded within the CRM application so that at a certain point in a process, a CRM user can quickly manually enter data or initiate a transaction in the other application from within CRM. This is useful if some user oversight or judgment must be applied in how the information is entered into the other application.

Types of Integration

Two types of integration are commonly seen in CRM projects: *data-level* integration and *user interface* integration. Scenarios exist where one is more appropriate than the other; your integration needs and the nature of your applications will guide you in selecting an approach.

Data-Level Integration

Data-level integration involves physically copying data from one application to the other. This type of integration is typically more involved to design, develop, and test. However, it has the advantage of making the data from one application fully available to all the functionality of the other. For example, if via integration we copy invoices from the accounting system into CRM, they are available for use in CRM reports, available to trigger notifications and other workflow rules in CRM, can be secured using the CRM security model, are able to be fed into e-mail messages generated into CRM, and so on.

One area to be defined for data-level integration is the direction that data will "flow"; for example, we have given examples where a customer record moved via the integration from the CRM application to the accounting application. What happens if someone updates the customer record, say by changing a phone number, in the accounting application? Should that change flow the other way and update the CRM record for that customer? Decisions must be made as to how data should flow through the integrations and which systems "master" which data (in other words, their version of the data is always considered "true" and overrides all other systems).

User Interface Integration

This form of integration involves embedding an element of one application's interface, or perhaps a report of data from the application, into another application. The data never physically moves from one application to the other; a *view* of it is simply presented to the user in the other application. This is useful when the key requirement is simply to show data to the user or to make it easier for them to initiate a transaction. This type of integration is simpler to design and develop than a data-level integration. To revisit our invoice integration example from the prior section, rather than implement a data-level integration to copy invoice data to the CRM application, we could develop a user interface integration, where a report of customer invoices from the accounting system is displayed in a tab on the CRM customer record. CRM users can view this information as if it were part of the CRM application. However, they could not query it via CRM search tools, and it could not participate in CRM workflow automation and other CRM features.

Integration Tools

For user interface integrations, typically the amount of custom programming required is small, and no integration tool is required. Most CRM applications include some capability for embedding external content in the user interface; the trend toward browser-based clients makes this even easier.

For data-level integrations, pure custom development is still an option, but the programming effort is much greater. Most organizations opt for implementing an off-the-shelf integration tool and then build their data integrations using it. The tool provides the low-level functionality (for example, error handling), connectors to common business applications, and a host of data transformation features to facilitate mapping and transforming data to move it from one application to another. The programming effort saved using one of these tools easily justifies its costs, and the result is easier to use and administer. Tool selection will be driven primarily by the type of integration needed, the applications involved, and your team's technology expertise and infrastructure.

Managing Data-Level Integration in CRM Projects

Integration efforts follow the familiar design-build-test-deploy of any CRM project, but in this section we will discuss some of the tasks specific to data-level integration work.

Identify Integration Scenarios and Applications Involved

The first step is to map out the desired integration scenarios, the direction of data flow, and the applications involved. This information can be concisely described with a table, as shown in Table 6-1.

Table 6-1. *Table of Integration Scenarios*

Application	Entity	Direction	Application	Entity	Triggering Event	Notes
Accounting	Customer	← →	CRM	Account	Account status in CRM changes to	No customer accounts will be manually

					"customer" and initiates insert into accounting. Changes in either application are reflected in the other.	created in accounting.
Accounting	Sales Order	← →	CRM	Order	Order status changes to "Submit to Accounting" and initiates insert into accounting. Status changes to sales order in accounting are reflected on the CRM order.	Once order flows from CRM to accounting, it should become read-only in CRM.
Accounting	Invoice	→	CRM	Invoice	Invoice is created in accounting.	Invoices are read-only in CRM.

Map Data

Once you have outlined the integration scenarios, you must develop a data map for each. This exercise is very similar to the data mapping required for a data migration effort; you can consider integration as a kind of ongoing data migration. For each scenario, you must define how fields from one application map to the other, and you must note any transformations required to the data as it passes from one system to another (Table 6-2).

Table 6-2. Integration Data Mapping

CRM Field	CRM Value	Accounting Field	Accounting Value	Notes
CRM Account←→Accounting Customer				
CustomerName		AccountName		
Street1		Address1		

Street2		Address2		
City		City		
..		..		
CRM Order←→Accounting Sales Order				
Title		Name		
Stage	New	Stage		
	In-Progress			
	Submit to Accounting		New	
	In Fulfillment		In Fulfillment	
..		..		

Developing the Integration

There are a few unique challenges associated with integration development that merit discussion; all of the tips for managing custom development work apply here.

One specific requirement for integration development is that the development team has a test instance of each application to be involved in the integration. This can be significant to set up and should be accounted for in your budgeting and scheduling for the integration work.

Integration Testing

As with the other components of a CRM project, there should be a documented test plan for integration. It's also especially important with integration to involve business stakeholders and subject-matter experts. It often takes people who are experts in the applications being integrated to CRM to spot problems with integrations.

Managing User Interface Integration in CRM Projects

User interface integration work is closer to standard custom development work than to data-level integration. There are a few unique challenges associated with designing and developing user interface integrations that merit discussion; all of the tips for managing custom development work apply here. One challenge that must be addressed for both user-level and data-level integrations is how to link data from one system to the other; this topic is described in the next section.

Linking Data Between Systems

A core challenge with developing integrations is how to link data from one application to another. For example, given an account record in the CRM application for the Jones Corporation, how can the integration program locate the record in the accounting system that represents the same organization? There needs to be some kind of *unique link* that tells the integration that record #123 in one application represents the same real-world entity as record #435 in a second application. As you have probably guessed, the name is not enough; what if the accounting system record is named Jones Corp?

One common solution to this challenge is to store the unique identifier from one application on the corresponding record in another system. The unique identifier, present in nearly all database applications, does just what you would think; it uniquely identifies a single record, just like a Social Security number uniquely identifies an American citizen. So, if Jones Corporation is record #123 in CRM and #435 in accounting, we can modify these systems to keep track of the identifier from the other, as shown in Figure 6-8.

CRM Application Record | Accounting Application Record

```
The Jones Corporation          Jones Corp
ID = 123                       ID = 435
Accounting ID = 435           CRM ID = 123
```

Figure 6-8. Managing unique identifiers

This system allows the integration process to correctly move data between applications. If several applications are to be integrated, it may make more sense to manage a separate table of unique identifiers rather than store this information with the applications themselves.

From the point that the integration is deployed, the integration process will manage typically unique identifiers for new records as they are created, either by populating identifiers from one system to another or by updating a separate table of identifiers. The potential challenge arises for the *existing* records in the two applications. The integration process likely needs to be able to link records together, to process updates, for example. So from the start, either all of the records in both applications must contain the identifiers from the other applications or the table of identifiers must be fully populated. In many cases, organizations have already solved this problem in some way and settled on some kind of approach to uniquely identifying records across systems. If your organization has not, your integration plans, budget, and schedule must factor in the time and effort to do so. Typically the majority of this work can be accomplished programmatically (for example, by name matching and by using address information, for example), but it requires error checking and handling of exceptions, which can be a painstaking manual process.

Reporting

Reporting is typically a central element of CRM engagements. Apart from its value as a productivity tool for users and as a mechanism for streamlining and automating business processes, the key value derived from CRM applications is the information needed to make better business decisions, and this information is most often accessed via a report.

Work on reporting appears across CRM project stages:

- *Envisioning*: During this stage, the high-level objectives for the project are defined. In many cases, reporting is central to one or more objectives. For example, objectives such as "Gain an objective measure of sales rep activity and performance" or "Understand support costs by product line" suggest that reports will be central to the solution.

- *Design*: During the design stage, the details of the needed reports will be defined, as well the business processes and application configurations needed to capture the information to feed the reports. For example, if a sales report requires opportunities to be categorized by size, when in the sales process will that information be captured, and by who? Where will they enter that information into the CRM application, and in what format? You can't consider report design independently of process and application design.

- *Build*: In this stage, reports are developed using whichever tool is appropriate for the type of report.

- *Deploy*: Reports should be included in both system and user acceptance testing to ensure that they are accurate and meet the needs of the CRM stakeholders. Reports should also be included in training, which should address not just the mechanics of how to run the reports but also the source and meaning of the data displayed.

What Makes an Effective Report?

Identifying suitable metrics or key performance indicators (KPIs) and designing effective reports is a subject of its own, and covering this topic in depth is outside the scope of this book. In another book, *Pro SQL Server 2008 Analytics: Delivering Sales and Marketing Dashboards*, Brian Paulen and Jeff Finken provide information on how to identify and evaluate KPIs. Here, we will offer a few guidelines to keep in mind when designing CRM reports. First, a good metric is one that fits well within your organization, taking into account your goals, the quality of your available data, and that it is easily understood by your team. This definition is shown effectively in figure 6-9.

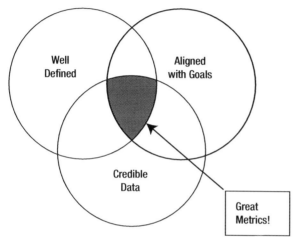

Figure 6-9. *What makes a good metric*

The following are a set of core principles that any organization can utilize to validate a set of foundational KPIs that can serve as the core business metrics for a comprehensive sales and marketing analytics program. For deeper information on the development of KPIs and their role in organizational strategy, the following are excellent resources: *Key Performance Indicators* by David Paramenter and *Balanced Scorecard Step-by-Step* by Paul Niven. For KPIs to be useful in driving business performance, you need to have a standard for what constitutes a good KPI. Further, the organization needs to have an awareness of this standard in order to be active participants in managing to the KPIs and refining them over time. These are core principles that we encourage clients to follow:

- The metric is specific.

- The metric is clearly owned by a given department or group.

- The metric is measurable.

- The metric can be produced in a timely manner.

- The quantity of KPIs must be limited to a manageable few items for a given scorecard.

- KPIs must have targets.

- KPIs must be aligned with the overall organizational goals.

Let's examine each of these principles in detail.

The Metric Is Specific

Specific means that the metric has a precise definition that can be easily explained and will be understood by any reasonable person within the organization. The most common example of a sales and marketing metric that fails the specificity test is forecasted revenue. This isn't to say that it is not important to have a measure for forecasted revenue, but this metric must be completely clear and must be well understood across the organization. For many organizations that we work with, we will ask what forecasted revenue is, and the response will be that obviously this is revenue associated with open deals that the sales team currently has in progress. This may be true, but it still lacks a great deal of specificity. A good, specific forecast revenue metric definition might be as follows: "The weighted value for all deals recorded in CRM that have been qualified and are expected to close this quarter. The value for all deals has been converted to U.S. dollars based on current exchange rates. This calculation can be completed by summing the forecast value and multiplying this amount by the close probability field in CRM." This is a good metric definition because it is unambiguous and detailed enough that any person familiar with the business and the key business systems can clearly understand what the value means once it is being produced at an aggregate level. Without a detailed definition like this, management meetings where these KPIs are being reviewed can easily devolve into questions about what the metric is intending to show (Does it include leads or only late-stage deals? Is this weighted based on close probability?), and valuable time that should be placed on the overall direction of the firm is lost making sense of the numbers.

The Metric Is Clearly Owned by a Given Department or Group

Ownership takes a metric from being merely interesting into something that will be acted upon. The key here is that in order for a metric to be useful in driving the organization forward, some individual or department must be accountable for it being on track. It may be interesting to know the rate at which maintenance is attached to product sales but is likely not relevant enough to be a KPI if no individual is clearly accountable for this attachment. By holding your metrics to a standard that there must be someone clearly accountable for them in order to spend time measuring and displaying them, you are performing one key filtering activity that will help you maintain your focus on a critical few metrics that truly drive the business.

The Metric Is Measurable

All elements that are intended to be displayed in a scorecard must be quantifiable. It is a great concept to measure employee satisfaction, but if there isn't a business process and system in place to track satisfaction both now and ongoing, it is not a relevant KPI because you simply can't use the metric in decision making without guessing. Perhaps you will identify a metric as critical, and this will lead you to define the process and systems around it in order to include it in your scorecard. This can be an excellent use of time and resources, but we strongly recommend against referring to metrics as KPIs unless you have in place the ability to measure them. This includes not only the systems to capture the metric but also the business processes that create consistency, audit tracking, and oversight.

The Metric Can Be Produced in a Timely Manner

One other seemingly small detail in the management of KPIs is paying attention to the time interval within which a metric can be tracked. If you have a weekly scorecard where two of the seven metrics are reported only monthly, those metrics are of questionable value. We do realize that not all measures will follow the same cadence, but we strongly recommend that in order for your KPIs to be useful in decision making, you must be able to repeatedly produce each metric in a routine consistent time interval so that it can be used in conjunction with the other key performance indicators to get an overall picture of the current state of the organization.

The Quantity of KPIs Must Be Limited to a Manageable Few Items for a Given Scorecard

One key client of ours asked us to review their management reporting. They called us in and with great pride displayed for us a 50-page manual that was produced monthly including metrics for virtually every operation in a 200-person department. They explained that the problems were that the book took too long to assemble (about 20 days), and that, unfortunately, it was not widely reviewed. The conclusion was that the current reports needed to be more automated, and there needed to be a big rollout of the new book so that people would know that they should refer to it in order to improve their performance. We asked the GM who owned the document if he referred to it on a regular basis. He said, "No, it's really just too much information for me to make sense of it. I don't have a full day to devote to figuring out what it all means." We agreed and recommended that we get to a point where each management tier in the organization would have a scorecard that is relevant for their role and captured and displayed metrics that they could control and influence. Each of these scorecards would display five to ten key metrics because we believed that was about the capacity of items on which any individual role could truly focus and impact. The key to this structure was that as you moved up the organizational ladder, the metrics in the scorecards were directly aligned with the organization's strategy. Many organizations assume that measuring as many business processes as possible makes for better performance, but we've found that the reality is almost the opposite. Organizations that carefully choose what to measure and selectively track only a relatively few metrics tend to have the most widely adopted and longest-lasting scorecard projects.

KPIs Must Have Targets

One of the areas where KPIs tend to break down is in moving from the theoretical measures that are developed at a strategy session to the practical management and tracking that occurs on a day-to-day basis. A key to success with KPIs is effectively moving from developing KPIs to setting and managing to targets based on the established KPIs. The keys to target setting are as follows:

- The designed target metric is captured within a set of existing business processes that are backed by systems where quantitative results are stored and accessible.

- Achieving or missing the target is within control of the department/person who is being measured by the scorecard.

- Targets are clearly time bound in a way that is aligned with the realities of the business and fits the organizational strategy. Many times we've seen good targets undermined by poorly designed software that either leaves the timeline unbounded for achieving a goal or evenly spreads a target across a series of months without taking into account seasonality that may affect many measures.

KPIs Must Be Aligned with Overall Organizational Goals

Recognize that the metrics can have only a positive, long-term impact if you have a clear organizational destination in mind (in other words, you'll have significantly different KPIs if your goal is to grow the organization by 50 percent annually and expand into new geographies than you will if your goal is to maintain 10 percent growth and maximize profitability). Teams that are developing KPIs must take great care to ensure that the selected metrics that are forward looking will actually lead toward the destination that the organization is looking to achieve. This statement may at first seem obvious, but it is a common failure for a team developing KPIs to become so enthralled with the process of developing creative metrics that they lose track of the need to deliver simple unambiguous metrics that are clearly linked with the organization arriving at a destination.

Report Sources

CRM reports are typically executed against the transactional database (the actual database used by the CRM application) or a separate database dedicated to reporting (often referred to as a *data warehouse*).

Reporting against the transactional database is the simplest approach; no data needs to be moved, and a separate database does not need to be maintained. However, there are several drawbacks to this approach:

- *Limited or nonexistent time-series data*: Information about how the data in your CRM application is changing over time is of potential business interest. However, reporting against the transactional database can provide only a snapshot of the data at the moment the report is executed. A data warehouse can accumulate trend data over time to answer questions that include a time dimension. For example, a transactional database report could answer the question "How large is my sales pipeline right now?" but not the question "How has the size of my sales pipeline changed in the last six months?"

- *Limited on nonexistent ability to integrate additional data sources*: Many reports need to draw information from multiple sources, including CRM, to provide a complete picture. CRM applications do not typically support importing data from other applications into their databases for reporting purposes.

- *Performance impact*: Reports often contain complex database queries and can tax the system on which they are run. This can impact the responsiveness and performance of the CRM application for all users.

Reporting against a separate data warehouse eliminates these issues but involves additional cost and adds complexity to the CRM project. The structure of the data warehouse must be defined, and then regular jobs must be created to synchronize new or updated data from the transactional database to the data warehouse. The reports run against the data warehouse are never in "real time," in the sense that they don't represent the current state of the transactional data, only the state at the time the data warehouse was last synchronized.

Selecting whether to use the transactional database or a data warehouse for CRM reporting is, like most decisions associated with a CRM project, a balance of business value, cost, risk, and complexity.

Reporting Tools

Several categories of reporting tools are available for CRM, for different purposes and with different characteristics. You may end up using a combination of tools to meet your reporting needs.

Presentation Reporting Tools

These tools excel at developing fairly static reports that are run regularly to address a recurring set of business questions and that are presented to decision makers. They typically yield visually appealing reports but with limited flexibility without changing the programming of the report and limited or no interactivity. Dashboard reports are specific, graphics-intensive versions of these reports.

Typically CRM applications include some basic presentation reporting tools that retrieve data from the transactional database as part of the application.

Data Analysis Tools

If presentation reporting tools are all about displaying the answers to predetermined business questions, data analysis tools are about exploring data to uncover trends and diagnose business issues *without* a specific question in mind. These tools predictably put less emphasis on a polished final result but include features to let an analyst filter and segment data, experiment with different visualizations, and perform statistical analysis.

Data analysis tools are not typically offered by CRM vendors and must be procured separately from business intelligence software vendors.

Designing Reports

Report design is ideally an iterative, collaborative process involving the business users, business analysts, and report developers. Central to the design process is the report specification document, which describes the functioning of the report and acts as the touch point of the process and ensures that everyone is on the same page.

There are a number of styles and variations of report specifications, but most will address the topics in Figure 6-10.

Report Specification

1. **Report Context**

    1.1.   **Name**

    1.2.   **Purpose**

    1.3.   **Key Users**

2. **Business Scenarios**

3. **Report Layout Wireframe**

4. **Data Sources**

5. **Table of Data Measures**

6. **Table of Data Dimensions**

7. **Report Filters and Parameters**

8. **Report Access and Security**

9. **Estimated Development Costs**

    It is helpful to describe the process used to identify the additional cost or schedule impacts.
    Ideally the process should be the same as the process used to estimate original project scope.

    9.1.   **Budget Impact**

Role	Hours
Project Manager	1
Developer	2
Analyst	3
TOTAL	6.0
TOTAL COST	$12,150

Figure 6-10. Sample reporting specification

Report Training

Given the tight budgets associated with CRM projects, it may be tempting to neglect training for reporting. There are several reasons why this is likely a mistake:

- Even if the report technology is simple and intuitive, training is typically needed on the *data*. Users need to understand what it means, where it came from, and how it was filtered on its way to the report. If the report includes complex calculations, these need to be spelled out for users. This information is critical to the user developing the trust in the report needed for the report to drive decision making.

- Report users are often senior executives who have a significant influence on the CRM program. Their satisfaction and enthusiasm are important to the success of the program and merit a training effort to ensure their experience is positive.

- Unlike presentation reports and dashboards, data analysis tools are complex software packages that require training to use effectively. You may consider sending your business analysts to specialized application training with your analysis tool vendor.

Data Migration

Data migration refers to the programmatic duplication of data from one application or system to another. It's an important element of many CRM projects. Consider an organization implementing a new CRM application: once the software is installed, the application is essentially empty. It contains no customer account, contact, or lead information. This information would have to be entered manually by the users as needed, gradually populating the CRM database, which is an arduous, inefficient, frustrating process. But most often an existing application has this customer information; perhaps it's an older CRM application that is being retired. A data migration effort uses software tools to copy this information from this existing application into the new CRM application so that when users start working in the new CRM application, most of their data is already there. This allows users to start productive work with a minimum of data entry of basic information and to have access to important historical information about their customers and prospects without having to refer to the retired application.

Data migration is not limited to new CRM implementation projects. As an example, an organization might want to retire an existing, stand-alone customer service application and expand their sales-focused CRM application to encompass the service functions. This project would likely involve a migration of customer and service history information from the service application into the CRM application so that service users could easily start using CRM to manage their work.

A well-executed data migration can be tremendously valuable, helping users make a smooth transition to a new application and saving countless hours of manual data entry. In cases with large data sets, data migration is the only practical way to populate the new application. However, data migration is often difficult, expensive, and imperfect. In this section, we will provide guidance on how to evaluate whether data migration makes sense for a given project and, if so, how to plan and execute a data migration effort.

Do You Need Data Migration for Your Project?

Because of the difficulty and expense associated with data migration, the sensible default is to not include it in the project and to add it only after careful consideration proves its merit. The business value of having the data in CRM must balance the effort to migrate it. Evaluate the following factors to determine whether a data migration is warranted:

- Does the relevant data exist in a structured format of some kind? Data migration can be accomplished from databases, spreadsheets, and other structured applications but is typically not feasible from unstructured data such as e-mail.

- How complex is the data? Multiple relationships within the data, free-form notes, and file attachments all complicate the migration.

- Size of the data set. For small, simple data sets, it may be more cost effective to have either users or temporary staff manually reenter data into the new application vs. executing a programmatic data migration.

- Availability of prior application post-project. If the source application is not being retired or can be made available post-project, it may make sense to not migrate data that will only occasionally be referred to by users.

- Quality of the data. If the data quality is sufficiently poor, it may be less effort to start from scratch than to migrate and then clean the data.

- Business value of the data. The value of having the data in question in the CRM application must be weighed against the costs associated with the migration.

Assessing Data Sources

Each data source (that is, application or database) being considered for migration must be examined from a number of different perspectives, both to enable a decision about whether to migrate it and to be able to design and execute the migration.

Data Access

The first hurdle to be overcome is data access; your data migration tool must be able to programmatically access the source application's data. Often there is a straightforward solution; data migration tools come packaged with "connectors" that allow them to easily connect to popular source applications. Or if the source application stores its data in a standard database (for example, SQL Server, MySQL, Oracle), most data migration tools can access it without difficulty. For data sources with obscure or proprietary data storage, data can often be accessed via some kind of export utility within the application, which will output the data into a standard format that can then be read by your data migration tool. If this is the case, it is important to make sure that this export feature includes the unique record identifiers used by the application to link records to one another (e.g., a contact record to its parent account record). If your data source uses a proprietary data storage format and does not include a usable export feature, your best bet may be to engage the application vendor's help in accessing the data.

Understanding the Schema

Once you can access the data, the real work begins. You must understand the structure of the data so that you can design your data migration process to copy the important data and preserve the relationships between the different types of data. Some applications have documentation, often as part of their software developer kit (SDK), that describes the data schema. If you are using an application's data export feature, this work is greatly simplified because you will typically export data one business entity at a time. If not, you will need to be a bit of a detective to decode the application schema. You are trying to determine, for each business entity (that is, account, sales opportunity), in which columns and tables the data is stored and how the relationships between different business entities are managed. Users of the application will be able to help by showing you how to navigate the application interface and highlighting what data is important and must be part of the migration, but they are not typically familiar with the data schema of the application. Selecting a few records of each type and switching between viewing the records via the application interface and within the data itself will typically illuminate the schema to a sufficient degree to enable the migration.

Data Quality

Several categories of data quality issues can dramatically increase the difficulty of data migration. Inconsistent application usage is perhaps the most prevalent; this may manifest itself as different users using the same application field to store different information, as well as different users using different interpretations of application terms (for example, one user would rate a particular lead as "qualified" where another would rate the same lead as "unqualified"), as well as simple intermittent usage (for example, only a subset of users ever bother to enter their prospect's mailing address). Other issues are straightforward but can take significant effort. For example, for free-text country fields in which some users have entered "United States," others "USA," others "U.S.A.," others "US," all variations must be handled by the data migration process. Spot-checking records, user interviews, and database queries can help assess the quality of the data in a source to determine the value of migrating it into the CRM application.

It is important to note as well that data quality can vary within a single application. For example, customer information may be rigorously maintained and updated, where lead information is used only by a small number of users with sloppy data entry habits and little standardization.

If possible, it is preferable to address quality problems first, independently of data migration. A common expression, "garbage in, garbage out," is often used to describe the fact that if the data fed into the migration process is of poor quality, then your CRM application will be populated with poor-quality data. Data migration does not solve data quality problems.

Designing the Data Migration

Designing the data migration has two parts. The first is a *functional* design, which describes what types of data will be migrated (by business entity, such as "accounts," "contacts," "service tickets"), which records of each type will be migrated (all, the last six months, or active records only?), and for each type, how the data will be mapped to the CRM application. The *technical* design describes how the migration will be accomplished, and its structure will be driven by the choice of migration tool. The technical design is outside the scope of this book; in this section, we will focus on the functional migration design.

Each source application that will be part of your data migration will require its own functional and technical design.

Data migration design, like application design (described earlier in this chapter), is a time-intensive process that requires participation of the project team members who understand the source applications and how they are used, as well as the finalized CRM application design.

Functional Design: Which Data to Migrate?

The project stakeholders and subject-matter experts familiar with the source application should be well equipped to provide guidance on the important business data managed by the application and what must be brought forward into CRM to meet the objectives of the project. The flip answer to this question that you may hear is "All of it, of course." In truth, each business entity added to the migration increases cost and complexity, and it is rare that all of the data in an application provides enough value to merit its inclusion in a migration process.

Functional Design: Which Records of Each Type?

The volume of data to be migrated impacts the cost and complexity of the data migration process. It can significantly increase the time needed to develop, test, and execute the migration. For each type of data identified as being part of the migration, consider whether the entire data set needs to be migrated or whether a subset is most valuable. In the example of migrating from one CRM application to another, you might ask yourself , "Do I need records of telephone calls with customers that happened over five years ago?" or "Are leads that have not been updated in more than two years really valuable?"

Functional Design: Mapping

Once you have identified the data types and the records within each type to be migrated, the next step is to document how the data will be mapped. This mapping is done at three levels, as described in the following sections.

Entity Mapping

Entity mapping is the highest-level mapping, where each type of source application data is mapped to a corresponding CRM business entity, based on the intent of the entity and the functionality it provides. Typically this mapping is straightforward and intuitive, but there can be mappings that require more consideration. For example, perhaps the source system has an entity called "Sales Call," where the destination has entities for "Meeting" and "Phone Call." A decision must be made as to where the Sales Call records will be mapped. Perhaps most of these represent physical meetings, in which case the decision might be made to map them to Meetings. Or perhaps there is a flag on the Sales Call to indicate whether the Sales Call was in-person or via phone, and this information is used to determine for each Sales Call whether to create a Meeting or a Phone Call.

The result of the entity mapping can be documented in a simple table like the one in Table 6-3.

Table 6-3. Data Migration Entity Mapping

Source Entity	CRM Entity	Notes
Customer	Account	All records.
Individual	Contact	All records.
Sales Opportunity	Sales Opportunity	All records modified since 1/1/2006.
Sales Call	Meeting Phone Call	If "In-Person" field is checked, create Meeting; otherwise, create Phone Call.

Field Mapping

Once the entity mapping is complete, you can proceed to the field-level mapping. This exercise consists of identifying, for each entity to be migrated from the source application, each data field to migrate and into which CRM field the data should be inserted. Ideally these mappings are simple; just take the value from field ABC in the source application, and insert it into field XYZ in the CRM application. However, as the quality of the data in the source application goes down, complexity begins to creep into the field mappings. Consider the case where some users in the source application put a certain piece of data in field ABC, while other users put the same data into field DEF. Now instead of a simple field-to-field mapping, you instead need to insert some logic, such as "look in field ABC first; if it is empty, then look in field DEF, and take the resulting information and copy it to field XYZ in the CRM application." And how do you decide what to do if a record in the source has data in *both* field ABC and field DEF? Ideally, you are starting to get a sense of why data migration can be such a difficult, imprecise, and expensive undertaking. Record ownership mapping is another complex element of the data migration. How should records belonging to former employees in the old application be assigned in the new application? Should you create user records for the former employees in the new application to try to preserve the record history, or should they all be reassigned to a current employee as part of the migration?

The field mappings can be documented by expanding Table 6-4.

Table 6-4. *Data Migration Field Mapping*

Source Field	CRM Field	Notes
Customer→Account		
CustomerName	AccountName	
Street1	Address1	
Street2	Address2	
Street3	Address2	Append to Address2
City	City	
..	..	
Individual→Contact		
FirstName	FirstName	
MiddleName	MiddleName	
LastName	LastName	
E-mail	E-Address1	
..	..	

Value Mapping

The final level of the mapping exercise is the value level. This is where we identify, for each row in our field mapping table, any transformation that needs to be made to the data in the source application before it is copied to the CRM application. Some examples of these "transformations" include the following.

Pick-List Mapping

This transformation is almost always required when mapping to a pick-list field in the CRM application. A pick-list field, also known as a drop-down list box or simply a list box, is a type of field where the user entering the information can select a single value from a limited set of options. The transformation is required for a couple of reasons. First, the contents of the fields to be mapped may not contain exactly the same values. For example, consider a field on a sales opportunity record to track the sales stage of the opportunity. In the old CRM application that is the source, the available options are "New," "In-Progress," "In-Contracts," "Won," and "Lost." However, the new CRM application includes a new sales methodology, with stages of "New," "Qualified," "Developing Solution," "Negotiations," "Won," and "Lost." In order to copy a sales opportunity from the source application to the new CRM application, we must define how the values for the sales stage from the source application should get translated to the CRM application. This definition requires input from the project team that is familiar with the source application and its data and the new CRM application design. These mapping can be documented by expanding the format of Table 6-5 to include field values.

Table 6-5. Data Migration Value Mapping

Source Field	Source Value	CRM Field	CRM Value	Notes
Customer→Account				
CustomerName		AccountName		
Street1		Address1		
Street2		Address2		
City		City		
..		..		
Sales Opportunity→Sales Opportunity				
Title		Name		
Sales Stage	New (3)	Sales Stage	New (8)	
	In-Progress (1)		Qualified (4)	
	In-Contracts (2)		Negotiations (2)	
	Won (4)		Won(1)	
	Lost(5)		Lost (3)	
..		..		

Even if the values line up perfectly for a given field between the source application and the new CRM application, a value mapping is likely needed. Applications typically do not store the actual text that we see in list boxes but rather a numeric code. So, for example, rather than store the word *New* in the database for an opportunity's sales stage, the application will store "3," which is the number associated with the word *New*. However, the CRM application likely has a different numeric code for "New," perhaps an "8." So even though the text options for the pick lists are the same between the two applications, we must change the "3" to an "8" when we copy it from the sales-stage field in the source application to the sales-stage field in the CRM application.

Data Lookups

Some fields require a data lookup to map from the source application to CRM. Consider, as an example, the "Sales Rep" field on the sales opportunity. The value in this field represents the salesperson who owns the opportunity. This field is typically a link to the appropriate record in a separate table of users within the source application. The migration process must take the value from the source application's sales opportunity table, look up the salesperson in this user table using this value, and then find the appropriate user value for that individual in CRM and enter their value in the appropriate CRM field.

Data Parsing

Different applications handle the same information in different ways; this can lead to the need to parse data as part of the data migration process. For example, consider a scenario where your source application stores an individual's name in a single field, called "name," but your CRM application has separate fields for each component of the name (for example, "first name," "middle name," and "last name"). The data migration process must somehow split the source data into its individual parts and pass the right part to the right field in CRM.

This is an example of where data migration can get messy and imprecise. While algorithms to break up names, as needed in the previous example, are good, they are not perfect and can make mistakes when presented with "Dr. Sally Brown" or "William Van Winkle." Is "Van" the middle name or part of the last name?

Data Migration Design Sign-Off

Once the data migration design is complete and documented, a formal sign-off by your team is important. This is an accountability point, and the team should understand that they are acknowledging they have reviewed and considered the design and that they believe it meets the business need. Data migration design is a detail-oriented task that requires patience. Time invested here is well spent, because changing the design once the process is built can require extensive rework and cost.

Data Migration Tools

Data migration can be accomplished using a variety of technology tools; in-depth coverage of these is outside the scope of this book. In this section, we will provide an overview of the two primary approaches, as well as some of the advantages and disadvantages of each.

Purpose-Built Application Data Migration Tools

A number of products are available that have been built specifically to help businesses migrate data in and out of enterprise applications such as CRM. These products have a number of compelling advantages that make them the best choice in most situations:

- Migrations are designed and executed via a user interface; no programming experience is required.

- Prebuilt connectors to popular applications can make setting up a basic migration very quick and easy if a connector is available for your application.

- They have a rich set of functions to easily perform data transformation as part of the data migration.

These applications can typically be licensed on a permanent basis for ongoing application integration (which requires similar tools as data integration) or on a temporary basis for a one-time data migration. Typically the developer or consultant time that is saved via the use of an off-the-shelf data migration tool far outweighs its license cost.

Custom Data Migration Tools

The other approach to data migration is to build your own migration application, either from scratch or using a platform technology such as Microsoft SQL Server Integration Services. If you have the development expertise available, this approach yields maximum flexibility and may be the only viable approach in unusual circumstances with uncommon data sources or special performance requirements.

However, it is far more labor-intensive than using an off-the-shelf data migration tool. Your developer will need to ramp up on the data schema or interface for the source application (to understand how to read data), as well as the interface for the CRM application (to successfully write the data from the source application). All of the logic that comes built into the off-the-shelf product, such as error handling, logging, transformation functions, may need to be written from scratch.

Testing the Data Migration: The Mock Migration

During the data migration development, your team will likely run a number of small migrations in your test environments to refine their migration process and spot problems. It is important, however, that at least one migration be executed with the full data set to be migrated. This "mock migration" acts as a test of the migration process, a gauge of migration performance and timing, and a dress rehearsal for the final data migration.

Some important elements of the mock migration are as follows:

- It should be executed using the full data set and on the same hardware that will be used to run the production migration. Part of the purpose for this exercise is to get a sense for the timing of the data migration; for large data sets, the migration process may take hours or even days.

- A cross section of the project team should be involved in testing and validating the results of the migration. Users close to the source application and its data will be in the best position to spot problems.

- The mock data migration procedure should be fully scripted beforehand, and a time-stamped log should be kept of every action taken. The time between the mock migration and the actual data migration may be weeks or months; you will not remember every step taken during the mock migration unless it becomes part of the script for the production migration.

There are several common approaches to validating the data migration process:

- *Review error logs of data migration tool*: This is a good place to start; most tools will log failed transactions that can highlight problems with the data migration process.

- *Query testing*: This type of testing involves running queries against both the source application and CRM to identify migration problems. For example, if the source application contains 50,000 account records, were 50,000 accounts created in CRM? If not, which records were not created and why? Queries can also be used to test specific pieces of the migration logic. For example, queries can provide a count of sales opportunities by sales stage in both the source application and CRM, allowing you to validate that your mapping logic was applied correctly.

- *Spot testing*: This involved identifying some number of records in the source application and checking them, field by field, against CRM to validate that all of the data was translated correctly and that the relationships between records in the source application were faithfully re-created in CRM. This is the only form of testing of the three that can be feasibly distributed across the project team.

When engaging the project team in testing, remind people to be *specific* when describing issues. Ideally, provide the specific records and fields that were not migrated correctly. General comments like "the data in CRM does not look right" are not helpful.

At the conclusion of testing the mock migration, you will need to make a go/no-go decision regarding the data migration process. If the issues uncovered in testing are minor and can be corrected easily and retested, you are likely ready to proceed. If the test migration uncovered significant issues, you may want to adjust your project plan to allow for a second mock migration after the issues have been addressed.

Planning the Actual Data Migration

The actual production data migration to populate a new CRM application in preparation typically occurs in the evening or over a weekend to minimize the impact to users. Ideally, the user community works in their old application until 5 p.m. on a Friday afternoon, and when they come into work on Monday morning, they begin using the new CRM application and find all of their data has been migrated; they can focus on coming up to speed on the new application, not on data entry.

In this "ideal" data migration model, 5 p.m. on Friday becomes the "cutoff" of the old application. If possible, the entire application is switched to "read-only" mode at this time, and an extract of the data is prepared to be used for the migration. The migration process is executed, using the same procedure as was used for the mock migration. Query and spot testing is performed to ensure that the process has been successful.

As you might imagine, many, if not most, CRM data migrations do not follow this simple pattern, and the particulars of your own migration will drive your own schedule and procedure.

The Data Migration Schedule

In addition to representing a final test of the data migration process and an opportunity to provide a go/no-go decision for the process, the mock migration provides an all-important sense of the duration of the migration process.

Ideally, the duration of the migration process will fit into a standard nonworking window such as an evening or weekend. If not, ideally the organization can accept some downtime to enable a sufficient window to execute the migration. If downtime is not an acceptable option, often data migration can be segmented to eliminate downtime and still allow users to be productive. For example, for the actual data migration, rather than bring over all five years of customer activity data (which might take four days to process and require downtime), one approach would be to migrate only the last year of data and then gradually migrate the older data in each successive nonworking window until all the data has been migrated.

The Script

Part of planning your data migration is to develop the detailed script, or series of tasks that will be executed in precise order, to complete the migration successfully. This script is created and refined during the technical development of the data migration process and validated by the mock migration. For the mock migration to have any value, the actual data migration must be executed in the *same way* using the *same script* as the mock migration.

Data Migration Summary and Key Lessons

The following are key lessons:

- Data migration is an important part of most CRM projects and can be tremendously valuable but should not be entered into unless justified by sufficient business value. It can be difficult, expensive, and imprecise.

- A common expression that you may have heard, voiced in regard to data migration, is "garbage in, garbage out." Data migration does not magically clean up, standardize, and deduplicate data; if your source applications have quality problems, data migration will simply move those problems into your CRM application.

- Don't outsource testing the data migration to your consulting partner; they do not have the context and understanding of the data and the source application to easily identify problems and sense when something doesn't "look right." Ensure that your team is involved.

Implementation Testing

For any enterprise application, testing is an important element of both the initial implementation project and all future development projects. Significant application bugs or downtime in enterprise applications like CRM can cripple business operations and have a tremendous negative impact; minor application bugs are an ongoing source of frustration, friction, and job dissatisfaction for users. A new application launch that is marred by significant bugs can put a black mark on the application that can impede adoption and degrade the value you hope to achieve for weeks and months after the issues are resolved.

While you will likely work with a consulting partner on the initial implementation of your CRM application and perhaps on subsequent enhancement projects, testing is one area where the work cannot be completely outsourced. Your consulting team can capably execute unit, system, integration, and performance testing, but they cannot take the lead on user acceptance testing. This is an area where your team's knowledge of your business, data, and processes is vital. A robust user acceptance test with engaged participation from representatives of each CRM stakeholder group is a key ingredient to a successful CRM project.

Types of CRM Application Testing

In this section, we will highlight the different types of testing that may be needed as part of your CRM project, their purposes, and how to integrate them into your project.

Unit Testing

This is the initial testing performed by a developer on a newly developed or enhanced application feature, as part of the development process, before flagging the feature as complete. This is a core responsibility of application developers and should be included in all CRM development as a natural part of the process. This testing should explore every possible logical branch of the feature to ensure that it is working as specified in the design. This testing is performed in isolation and is not expected to test the interplay of different features with one another.

System Testing

Once the development of all the CRM application features is completed and they are deployed in a test environment, system testing ensures that they mesh with one another and still function properly in the presence of the complete feature set. Often individual features can impact one another in ways that individual feature developers do not foresee, so testing the complete feature set together is vital. System testing is typically executed at the end of the build stage of the CRM project life cycle, when all features have been developed and unit tested.

Integration Testing

In many organizations, the CRM application is integrated into other business applications such as accounting or provisioning. Integration testing in intended to validate that the application linkage is functioning properly and that data is flowing from one application to another and being translated correctly if needed.

Performance Testing

Less important for CRM application deployments with minimal custom development, but critical for those with significant custom development, is performance testing. Large data sets and large numbers of users can have an unexpected and deleterious effect on CRM application performance, resulting in sluggish response times, timeout errors, and frustrated users. A geographically dispersed user community can also trigger performance problems with CRM applications, because network connections between countries can be poor and impact communications between CRM clients and servers. If your project includes significant custom development and one or more of the aggravating factors of data volume, high user counts, or geography, ensure that your project team has included performance testing in their project plan.

The emphasis on custom development for performance testing stems from the fact that the test cases used by the major CRM application vendors likely include both large data sets and large numbers of simultaneous users (assuming you are using an application designed for your size of organization). The standard application, running on appropriate hardware, has likely already been tested and passed in scenarios more rigorous than your own. Custom development, on the other hand, has never been tested, and there are many ways for a developer to author code that fails under high load.

User Acceptance Testing (UAT)

User acceptance testing is a critical validation step in a CRM project life cycle. Prior to user acceptance testing, all CRM components have passed unit and system testing, and all data has been migrated. The test environment is, at this point, essentially identical to the production environment post-launch. User acceptance testing involves exercising the key business scenarios to be supported by the CRM application to validate the following:

- All features described in the approved application design documentation function as the design team intended.

- The application, as designed and developed, meets the project goals and is ready for launch.

A unique feature of user acceptance testing is that it is executed by a set of application users themselves: sales managers, perhaps, or customer service representatives. All testing to this point has primarily been conducted by the technical team. User testing is also unique in its all-encompassing nature; application features, migrated data, integrations, and other application areas are all examined as part of the user test.

Developing Test Plans

Thorough test plans explore and validate all logical branches of an application and all-important business scenarios. They should be written with sufficient details such that they can be executed reliably and consistently by multiple individuals.

System Test Plans

System test plans are made up of test cases; each test case includes the following elements, often arranged in a tabular structure and grouped by functional area:

- ID is a unique identifier for each test case.

- Actions describe the precise steps within the application that the tester should execute.

- Expected Result describes what the outcome of the actions should be to allow the tester to evaluate whether the application passed the test case or failed.

- Pass/Fail indicates whether the application outcome matched the expected result.

- Actual Result describes, for a failed test, the behavior exhibited by the application.

- Test Date/Time is the date and time the test case was executed.

- Tester is the individual executing the test case

- Environment describes the technical details of the environment used for the test, such as which test environment, test client machine, and so on.

- Comments are additional descriptive notes regarding the test case.

Figures 6-11 and 6-12 show a sample system test plan, both before and after testing.

2   Testing Scenarios – User Interface Use Cases

2.1   Use Case 1

ID	Action	Expected Results	Actual Result	Pass / Fail	Test Date / Time	Tester Initials	Environment	Comments
1	Create new customer record. Set State field = "Oregon"	Customer record should be auto-assigned to Sally Jones, the Oregon sales rep.						
2	Create new sales opportunity. Leave sales stage field blank.	Application should block save, and prompt user with message to provide a sales stage						
3								
...								

2.2   Use Case 2

ID	Action	Expected Results	Actual Result	Pass / Fail	Test Date / Time	Tester Initials	Environment	Comments
1								
2								
3								
4								
5								
...								

Figure 6-11. Sample system test plan (prior to testing)

1 Testing Scenarios – User Interface Use Cases

1.1 Use Case 1

ID	Action	Expected Results	Actual Result	Pass / Fail	Test Date / Time	Tester Initials	Environment	Comments
1	Create new customer record. Set State field = "Oregon"	Customer record should be auto-assigned to Sally Jones, the Oregon sales rep.	--	Pass	4/5/2011 2:00PM	Bob	TEST02	--
2	Create new sales opportunity. Leave sales stage field blank.	Application should block save, and prompt user with message to provide a sales stage	System blocks save and prompts user, but error message makes no sense.	Fail	4/5/2011 2:10PM	Bob	TEST02	We should get Joan to review all the error messages.
3								
4								
5								
6								
7								
...								

1.2 Use Case 2

ID	Action	Expected Results	Actual Result	Pass / Fail	Test Date / Time	Tester Initials	Environment	Comments
1								
2								
3								
4								
5								

Figure 6-12. Sample system test plan (after testing)

User Acceptance Test Plans

User acceptance test plans differ in format from system test plans, to reflect the different perspective and goals of this type of testing. User acceptance testing is not really about finding "bugs" but rather about validating that the CRM application as configured supports the business process and meets the goals of the application. The business users who provide the key input during the CRM application design stage may lack the experience with applications to foresee in detail how the finished application will work; user acceptance testing lets them validate that the application "works" and will elegantly support users in accomplishing their work. Given this focus, user acceptance test plans are built around key business scenarios like those in Figures 6-13 and 6-14. You may find that facilitating a user acceptance test is equal parts training and testing, as users often require some level of training to be able to effectively test and assess the application's readiness.

1   Testing Scenarios – User Acceptance Testing

1.1   Use Case – Lead Management

ID	Scenario	Process / Application Steps	Pass / Fail	Tester	Date / Time	Comments
1	Qualify Lead	1. Contact lead via phone 2. During discussion: 　　a. Provide an overview of our services 　　b. Ascertain whether a project has been established, with a budget and schedule 　　c. Ascertain name of project sponsor/decision-maker 3. Enter call notes into CRM notes area 4. Enter budget into *Project Budget* field on CRM Lead 5. Create a contact record for the project sponsor and link it to the Lead. 6. If project exists, budget > $50,000, set lead *Status* field to "Qualified" – otherwise set this field to "Nurture" 7. If Lead is set to "Qualified" it will be auto-assigned to the appropriate field sales rep.				
...	...	...	...	...	...	...

1.2   Use Case – Opportunity Management

ID	Scenario	Process / Application Steps	Pass / Fail	Tester	Date / Time	Comments
1						
...	...	...	...	...	...	...

Figure 6-13. User acceptance test plan (prior to testing)

1   Testing Scenarios – User Acceptance Testing

1.1   Use Case – Lead Management

ID	Scenario	Process / Application Steps	Pass / Fail	Tester	Date / Time	Comments
1	Qualify Lead	1. Contact lead via phone 2. During discussion: 　　a. Provide an overview of our services 　　b. Ascertain whether a project has been established, with a budget and schedule 　　c. Ascertain name of project sponsor/decision-maker 3. Enter call notes into CRM notes area 4. Enter budget into *Project Budget* field on CRM Lead 5. Create a contact record for the project sponsor and link it to the Lead. 6. If project exists, budget > $50,000, set lead *Status* field to "Qualified" – otherwise set this field to "Nurture" 7. If Lead is set to "Qualified" it will be auto-assigned to the appropriate field sales rep.	PASS	Holly	4/15/2011 10:00AM	When lead status is set to "Nurture", it would be great for it to drop off the salesperson's list of active leads.
...	...	...	...	...	...	...

1.2   Use Case – Opportunity Management

ID	Scenario	Process / Application Steps	Pass / Fail	Tester	Date / Time	Comments
1						
...	...	...	...	...	...	...

Figure 6-14. User acceptance test plan (after testing)

Implementation Training

Often under-prioritized but critical to a successful CRM program is training. Each time your CRM program changes, whether it is a process or the application change, training must be considered. Training helps ensure that your team is executing business processes correctly and using the CRM application consistently and in a way that allows them to maximize their productivity. Even absent any changes, training is still an important and ongoing element of your CRM program, because you will still need to train new hires and people who are changing job roles.

Goals of Training

The obvious goal of training is to ensure that the people in your organization understand the customer-facing processes that they will need to execute or support as part of their jobs and that they can confidently use the CRM application in the context of these processes. New processes and applications can be confusing and intimidating, so a formal training program, where users are led through the new material and have an opportunity to ask questions and discuss exception cases, is valuable and will be more successful than leaving people to fend for themselves or relying on informal "on-the-job" training.

Another important goal of training is to promote consistent application of the CRM processes and consistent usage of the CRM application. Both the processes and application are more valuable when used consistently, and this requires getting everyone on the same page. Formal training is an excellent way to accomplish this.

Elements of a Successful Training Plan

As with most elements of your CRM program, success with training begins with a well-thought out plan. In this section we'll describe several elements of an effective training plan.

Address Both Process and Application

A common shortcoming of CRM training is to focus, sometimes exclusively, on the CRM application. Thinking that the application is what is new/different/intimidating, the organization's training content focuses on topics such as logging into the application, searching for customer information, entering different types of interactions (orders, opportunities), and executing reports.

The shortcomings from this application focus become apparent as users begin production use of the application and result in questions, confusion, and inconsistent usage. User will make comments similar to "I know *how* to convert a new lead to a qualified opportunity but *when* should I do so?" or "How do I determine whether a service case should be flagged as *urgent*?" These questions indicate a lack of clarity on the process and terminology associated with the application, not the mechanics of its usage.

The best training walks users step by step through the processes they will need to support for their job function and demonstrates at each step what actions need to be taken in the CRM application. Common exceptions and how to handle them should also be discussed.

Define Your Terms

Confusion over terminology, and the resulting inconsistent or incorrect usage of the CRM application, is a common problem with CRM programs. Ensure that as part of your training content you define unambiguously any terms used within the application and strive in your CRM application design to avoid using terms differently in different contexts. You may also want to include this information in your training materials so that users can reference it later when they have questions.

Multiple Training Exposures

Repeated exposure to training material helps people "lock in" their understanding. Don't rely on a single isolated training session as the entirety of your training program. Ideally, spread the content over a couple of sessions to avoid a long session where people's attention span falters and to provide an opportunity to repeat critical elements. Make sure there are opportunities for informal follow-up training or question-and-answer sessions at regular intervals after the primary training.

Tailor Training for the Audience

Trainees will be most engaged if the content being presented is specific to their own job function. Rather than delivering generic training or including role-specific content that applies only to a subset of the training audience, it is better to deliver multiple training sessions, with each targeted at a specific role. It may be possible to cover some topics in a generic session and then have people break out into separate sessions by role for more specific content.

Include Exercises and Examples

Hands-on exercises help uncover questions and areas of confusion from training participants, build their application familiarity and therefore their confidence, and break up the training session. While setting up hands-on exercises is a bit more involved from a training infrastructure standpoint (machines running the CRM application must be made available at the training venue), our experience is that this effort is justified by the increased quality of the training. Examples of common situations, especially around exception cases, are helpful additions to the training content as well.

Executive Participation

For new CRM program launches, training will be most people's introduction to the program and the CRM application. In our experience, it has helped to have the program's executive sponsor introduce the training, by describing for the participants why the organization is launching a CRM program, the benefits that it should realize by doing so, and what will be required from the training participants for the program to be successful. As we have discussed at other points in this book, continued, vocal support for CRM from the organization's leadership team is important to successfully driving adoption. Training is an excellent opportunity for this.

Don't Forget Help

Make sure your training informs participants of the different options for support after training is complete. This may include an e-mail distribution list for questions, superuser "office hours," or help and training content on an intranet site.

Training Approaches

We'll describe next the two most common approaches to CRM program training that we have seen: live classroom training and webinar-style training. There are others, such as online self-guided training, but these two are the most common and most cost-effective that we have seen used regularly.

Classroom Training

This is the classic, live, instructor-led training. We have found it to be the most effective approach for training. Ideally, the content will blend lecture, presentation, application demonstration, and hands-on exercises for participants. Group size should be kept to 15 or less to ensure that the session is interactive and that the instructor can give each participant some individual attention if needed. Sessions should be no longer than four hours, with plenty of breaks.

Hands-on exercises typically mean that training participants will have either their own laptop computer or a training room computer in front of them during the training session. These exercises should be tightly controlled to limit the use of the computers to the exercise time only to help keep the participants focused on the training content and avoid them getting immersed in their e-mail or other work.

Organizing live classroom training can be difficult and expensive for geographically dispersed organizations. We have seen organizations successfully deliver training by aligning it with preplanned events such as national sales meetings, where all the impacted employees are already planning to convene.

Web Training

Web training is easier to organize and less expensive (no travel costs) than live classroom-style training. It can be easily recorded for reuse. However, it has several disadvantages. Interactions between instructor and participant are more difficult. Participants often "tune out" and work on side projects or catch up on their e-mail during training. The instructor cannot read faces or body language and may "lose" the audience without knowing it. The logistics of hands-on exercises may be more complex, because software may need to be installed on remote users PCs rather than on a set of machines in a training room.

Training Resources

A well-designed set of training resources will make your training sessions more effective and provide participants with materials they can reference for help as they adjust to new processes and the new or enhanced CRM application.

Guides

The training guides should be role-specific and organized to walk readers step by step through each business process, with reference to the corresponding actions required in the CRM application. Screenshots are an important element and will make the guidance on application usage much easier to understand. Training guides should also include some kind of "organization dictionary" or in some fashion should define all of the terms employees might encounter.

Training guides should also be kept up-to-date; any time a process changes or the CRM application is enhanced, the affected text and screenshots in the training guides should be updated.

While often prepared as a simple document, there are advantages to making the training guide content available online to users within a collaboration tool such as a wiki. This allows users to search the guide easily, to add comments, and even to update the guide with additional information.

Figure 6-15 shows a sample table of contents for a simple, sales-focused training guide.

Table of Contents

1 OVERVIEW 5

1.1 CRM Concepts 5
1.2 Starting CRM 5
1.3 Where to Go for Help 6
1.4 Layout and User Preferences 8

2 FILTERING, SORTING, AND SEARCHING 12

2.1 Filtering and Sorting 12
2.2 "Look for" Search 13
2.3 Pre-Defined Views 14
2.4 Advanced Find / Custom Views 14
2.5 Drilling Down (or Up) on Related Information 16
2.6 Activity Management (E-mail, Phone Calls, Tasks, Appointments, etc.) 16
2.7 E-mail 17
2.8 Managing Activities 20
2.9 All Other Activities (Phone Calls, Tasks, Appointments, Letters, etc.) 21
2.10 Notes 28

3 ACCOUNT MANAGEMENT 29

3.1 Account Definition 29
3.2 View Accounts 29
3.3 Creating and Editing Accounts 30

4 OPPORTUNITY MANAGEMENT 36

4.1 Create Opportunities 36
4.2 Edit Opportunities 38
4.3 Finding Opportunities 39
4.4 Deactivate / De-Dupe / Delete Account 39

5 CONTACT MANAGEMENT 41

5.1 Create a Contact 41
5.2 Edit a Contact 42
5.3 Deactivate / De-Dupe / Delete Contact 43

6 MARKETING 45

6.1 Quick Campaigns 45
6.2 Campaigns 47

7 REPORTS 52

7.1 Advanced Find 52
7.2 Reports 52
7.3 Excel Worksheet and Pivot Table Reports 52

Figure 6-15. *Sample training guide table of contents*

In addition to a more standard training guide, many organizations find value in focusing on commonly asked questions. We have historically utilized a quick-reference guide as a tool for providing this type of information. It is helpful if this tool is printable and potentially able to be laminated so that users can post it in their office or carry it with them in a computer bag. While yours will be specific to the application you choose to implement, Figure 6-16 is one example of what a quick-reference guide might look like.

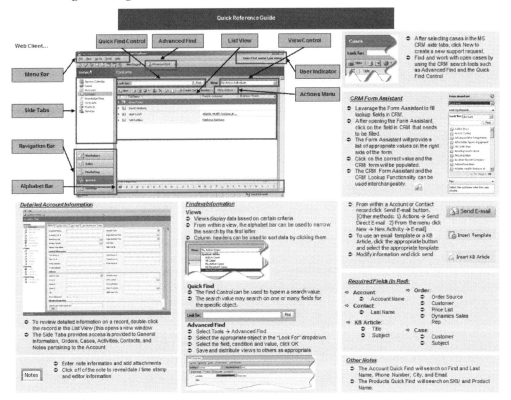

Figure 6-16. *Sample quick-reference training guide*

Recorded Demonstrations

Recorded demonstrations show the application screen, while a user navigates to perform certain tasks and provide a voice-over commentary of their actions. These videos are straightforward to make and do not require expensive equipment or software. Recordings can be made of common scenarios (for example, "Creating a service ticket" or "Adding products to an order") and posted on a intranet site or a training wiki for viewing by application users.

CRM Team Meetings

It's helpful when launching a CRM program to schedule regular CRM team meetings. These sessions can be used for informal training and for people to describe questions, problems, or frustrations they are experiencing with the CRM program. These are a great venue to keep a finger on the pulse of the employees with respect to CRM and to understand how the processes and application can be enhanced to provide a better experience. It also provides a venue for people to help each other with CRM questions, which serves to solidify a sense of shared ownership over the application that can help user adoption.

Ongoing Training

Training is an ongoing part of your CRM program. Although there are spikes in training activity associated with CRM projects that change processes or enhance your CRM application, there must be a regular training schedule for existing employees to brush up on areas where usage is inconsistent or incorrect and to brief users on new areas of the CRM application that may increase their productivity. In addition, there will be turnover in your organization, and new employees and employees changing roles will require training.

New-hire training is typically delivered by designated trainers within each functional area. Seek individuals with a deep understanding of the group's processes, an appreciation of the value of CRM to the group and organization, and the soft skills to communicate and train effectively. The CRM administration team is best equipped take the lead on regular training for users on new or unused CRM application capabilities.

Launching the Solution

Once you have completed all the necessary training activities, you should begin to focus on the deployment of the initial phase of functionality. During this process, you should expect some pain throughout both your team and your organization. The new application will likely be a cause of significant change to your users regardless of what they used in the past. Being prepared for the pain, and more importantly to assist your users with the transition process, will allow you and your team to successfully drive the project to completion.

Cutover

The cutover (or go-live) process is one that will vary greatly depending on the type and complexity of implementation. The most important thing to focus on around cutover is planning and communication. Understanding who is doing what and when they're doing it will mean a much smoother process. The process of taking the application live can be stressful, with tight timelines and a multitude of tasks to complete.

While we provide a similar example in Chapter 7, the template provided in Figure 6-17 will allow you to track go-live tasks, the person responsible, and the time that the task needs to be complete. While you may not always hit the appropriate date and time, planning all tasks in this manner will allow you to see the big picture.

CRM
Go-Live Plan

Task	Responsible Party	Required Completion Date	Required Completion Time	Completed (Initial)
Pre Implementation				
Implementation				
Post Implementation				

Figure 6-17. Sample CRM go-live plan

Depending on whether you are migrating from another application, you may be required to complete the various go-live activities over a weekend. This will allow you to work through the process while providing little interruption as possible to your user community.

Next, we will highlight a few of the key components to focus on as part of the go-live process.

Final Data Migration

As we discussed earlier in this chapter, it is best if the go-live data migration occurs during nonworking hours. Not only does this minimize interruptions for your users, but it will make the process of migrating the data, and testing its accuracy, much easier. At a high level, this process will consist of clearing out any work done during test data migrations, executing the production migration, monitoring the migration completion, and validating the data once the migration is complete. Consider involving users in the data validation process to ensure they have a stake in certifying the validity of the data.

As we just mentioned, completing this process over the course of a weekend is a preferable approach. If you are unable to use weekend time to complete this work, you will need to include time in your plan to perform an initial migration, validate the data, and then complete a migration including the deltas between the initial migration and the work completed during the intervening period.

Client Application Installation

Depending on the CRM application you use, some may offer you the opportunity for you to implement a client user interface or add-in product as part of the implementation. These days, based on the importance of e-mail in most corporate environments, many of these client installations occur within your e-mail application and provide users with a seamless way to manage information between your CRM application and their e-mail. If this installation is something you need to focus on, consider the following items:

- *Who does the install?*: The obvious choices for performing your installation are the end users themselves, your internal IT team, or the vendor assisting you with your implementation. While each of these has some benefit, typically your internal IT team will have the most familiarity with your internal infrastructure and can likely perform the installation quickly. Given their familiarity with the client, your vendor may be able to assist quickly, but the cost-to-value equation may make this a secondary or tertiary option.

- *Install prerequisites*: Most of the applications requiring an install will have software prerequisites that are required to be installed prior to the actual client application installation. In addition to the physical installation, you should spend time validating whether your end users' computers are sufficiently powerful to support the client installations. Unfortunately, many corporate IT environments purchase the bare-minimum computers for their users, and hardware issues can cause significant performance issues jeopardizing application adoption following the initial go-live period.

- *Deployment approach*: Depending on how savvy your IT team is, you may be required to install these clients one by one. In larger, more accomplished IT environments, deployment tools may be available to push these updates out to client machines and lessen the burden on the internal IT or vendor staff. If you do end up using this approach, spend a little time validating the initial settings with the IT team to ensure your user community gets the client correctly the first time.

While these considerations are important to evaluate if using an application with a required or optional client application, you can avoid many of these complications by using a web-based application. Depending on the CRM selected, there may be restrictions on the browser version allowed, but the process should be much more straightforward.

Communications

During the cutover process, providing a dependable stream of communications to various constituencies will aid your team should any issues arise and will also provide any necessary air cover should things come up requiring attention of your project leadership team or user community.

Consider providing updates once or twice a day depending on the duration of your cutover process. Use these updates to communicate status, address any issues that have come up, and interject an interesting feature for your user community to review.

Figure 6-18 shows a simple but effective template you could use to provide these updates.

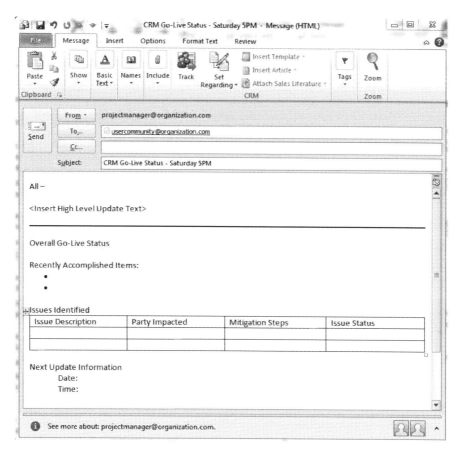

Figure 6-18. Sample go-live user communication

In addition to the normal user updates, if any issues arise, communicating those before they become significant will make the success of your go-live more likely. In addition to soliciting support as quickly as possible, having your project leadership team involved in any crucial issues or decisions will allow them to participate more actively.

Post-deployment Support

Once you have completed the go-live process and deployed the application, you need to switch into application support mode. As part of your deployment, you should expect to spend some amount of time with users answering questions or providing information on how to use specific components of the application. Chapter 7 deals with this support from a longer-term perspective, but planning for short-term needs is also important.

If you engaged a vendor in the project, they will also likely include some time to support you and your users during the time immediately following go-live. Regardless of who owns the task, review the items outlined in Chapter 7 and select those that make sense for your implementation.

Initial Application Management

Like post-go-live support, ongoing application management is covered in more detail in Chapter 7. That said, identifying a few focal points for you to think through immediately following deployment is important. In this section, we will highlight a few of the early considerations.

Driving Adoption

Driving adoption quickly as part of your CRM implementation will mean the difference between a quick go-live with the potential for positive press and an ugly slog through user issues and complaints. Making sure users see the appropriate value in the application, and are using it fully, will help keep things positive. One common mistake organizations make is allowing users to continue to use or view an old application following the deployment of the new CRM tool. This is one of the most significant errors an implementation team can make because it provides an opportunity for excuses from the user community and will cause nothing but confusion. Of course, if you are going to turn off a previous system, you need to spend the appropriate amount of time ensuring data and needed functionality from the old system is available. In addition, visible and vocal senior executive support during the initial period after launch is important to help users keep the value and vision of CRM in mind and to encourage employees to keep at it until they get comfortable with the new processes and application.

The Carrot vs. Stick Approach

To ensure adoption of the delivered solution, senior executives can choose between the "carrot" and the "stick" approach. While both of these approaches have merit, the decision on direction depends on management style and the existing adoption of other applications within an organization. Based on our experience, few managers have the stomach to make the "stick" work in the absence of "carrots," so keep that in mind as the go-live process progresses. "Carrots" may include recognition of users who are embracing the application or small bonuses for helping evangelize the application. An example of a "stick" (for a sales team) might be a policy whereby commission is not paid on won deals unless they were recorded and tracked in the CRM application.

Tying KPIs and Compensation to CRM Usage

One of the more prevalent ways of using the stick to drive application usage is tying an individual's objectives or compensation to CRM usage. Whether the CRM usage you are looking for is as simple as tracking e-mail correspondence or activity or as complex as providing detailed sales stage and status information on sales opportunities, you should be able to successfully find unquestionable metrics to use to govern compensation. Consider defining an algorithm that factors in usage, number of records updates, and number of activities tracked and producing a per-user score. You can also make sure that users get paid commission only on opportunities that were in the system for a specific period of time. This will prevent someone from entering information only when they get a signed contract.

Change Management

Like most of the topics in this section, change management is discussed more heavily in Chapter 7. Immediately following go-live, it is important to leverage the tools we provide in Chapter 7 to track any immediate feedback about the application. You may want to schedule steering committee discussions regularly following go-live, potentially even daily for 10 or 15 minutes to discuss any high-priority issues that come up. The steering committee should be prepared to review issues and update the team quickly with progress and mitigation steps (if appropriate). Additionally, consistent communication about the status of the application, benefits provided by the new tool, and highlights of key features will enable you to drive a more positive outlook and be more responsive to any concerns raised by the team.

People Management: New Job Functions

CRM implementation in and of themselves will not change how your people function; it may require them to operate differently within the purview of their current job. Perhaps people used to hand paper orders to someone in accounting for processing and will now enter them themselves in CRM. Perhaps users formerly had to spend a significant amount of time reporting pipeline status, but that process is now automated. Whether they have additional time to spend on high-value pieces of their job or have slightly different workflows associated with day-to-day tasks, you should be prepared to support them as much as needed during the transition period.

Pulling It All Together: Sample CRM Implementation Project Plan

In this chapter, we've organized content by topic, such as data migration, reporting, and so on, rather than by how you will organize the work of your project chronologically. In Figure 6-19, we've laid out a high-level project plan to help illuminate this second perspective: how the project work is actually laid over a calendar and completed.

Here are some important notes about the diagram:

- The iterative project process that we have discussed is depicted. Design work continues well into the iterative build stage as adjustments are made based on the project team's interactions with prototypes of the CRM application.

- Since they are ultimately dependent on the design of the application, the report, integration, and data migration designs will likely change somewhat after the initial design phase in the iterative approach to reflect changes made to the application during the iterations. All other designs cannot be "chipped in stone" until the application design is finalized.

- Items are not listed within each stage in a specific order to reflect the sequence of their completion.

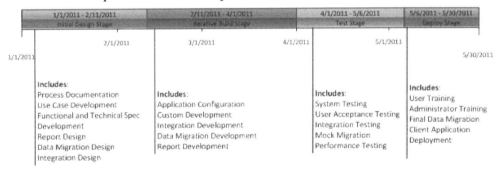

Figure 6-19. High-level project plan

Common Project Issues and How to Avoid Them

Now that we have provided you with an overview of the various processes and tools that can be used to help you implement your CRM application, we wanted to outline a few of the classic project issues that arise with CRM implementations. We will provide a few of the symptoms or causes of these issues and a bit of information on steps you can take to avoid them.

Over-scoping

At various points in this book, we talk about using a phased or big-bang approach to CRM. Over-scoping is another way of articulating the same challenge. Allowing too much scope, or scope that collectively requires too much change, into your CRM implementation will provide significant challenges to you as you roll out the first version of your CRM application. It isn't just the volume of scope that defines whether a solution is over-scoped but the complexity of the scope as well. If you include numerous integrations, multiple system replacements, or other complex items, your user community could become overwhelmed by the change.

Focusing on small, manageable deployments is the easiest way to mitigate the risk of over-scoping. If you can, break the first phase of the implementation into a small, meaningful set of scope that provides distinct value to the end user community. Once you've had a successful phase, finding more time, budget, and success should be a straightforward process. If you do need to do a large implementation as part of the first phase, critically review the scope items to ensure that no one user group is over burdened by the change. You can also devote extra time to training and user support to help alleviate any of the extra risk added by a larger scope volume.

Overly Complicated Design

Whether you are simply designing the account and contact entities or are focused on a broad set of custom entities and attributes in your CRM application, trying to make them all things to all people can quickly cause conflict when it comes to the form layout and usability. This conflict exists whether looking at CRM forms or the complexity of integrations and custom items in your CRM program. Building too much up front or not carefully managing the expectations of users can cause the design and, ultimately, the implementation of your CRM system to become too complex and will cause issues with user adoption.

We often hear our customers and other consultants talk about using out-of-the-box functionality whenever it is available. This is absolutely one place to start when looking to avoid an overly complicated design of your CRM application. In addition to focusing on native CRM features, having someone involved in the project who can objectively look at the various requests for customization or automation and provide guidance on what to build initially will help ensure your design both meets users' needs and remains as uncomplicated as possible.

Software-Driven Projects

A common mistake most organizations make is allowing the features available in various CRM applications to drive the overall implementation. Whether they change an existing, working process to fit within the new CRM tool or implement a feature just because it is available in the tool, this immediately puts the adoption of the tool at risk. Any time users are required to change a process for the sake of technology, they are more likely to rebel against the application and look for workarounds to the new application. Additionally, this approach often leads to over-scoping, which will cause many of the same issues.

With the technology available today, virtually anything can be customized or built into your CRM application. Focus on using the tools to make the application fit your organization's desired processes. We recognize that endlessly building things into your CRM tool is both costly and time-consuming, so it may be important to prioritize items that do the most to facilitate processes, but eventually, with the right focus and continued dedication, you will eventually implement all the necessary functionality to meet all the process requirements.

Lack of Executive Support

At virtually all points throughout your project, having the appropriate level of executive support is crucial to finding the right vendor (if appropriate), helping set the implementation team's priorities, and guiding the overall project. Following the initial deployment, executive support is critical to helping drive user adoption for the solution and ensuring any issues that arise are both communicated appropriately and dealt with in the appropriate way. If at any point the support from the executive team, or even just the level of communication, begins to wane, this will represent a risk to your project that should be dealt with quickly.

Managing any issues that arise around the level or amount of executive support is generally pretty straightforward. Fortunately, most executives respond when presented with a risk that will cost them either money or trust, so simply raising the issue will often raise the level of participation. If that alone does not work, look for opportunities to help them with things like communication by drafting project e-mails. Finally, ensuring that they have all the necessary information at hand when talking about the value of CRM or are addressing any issues will make them much more likely to participate heavily in the process.

Managing Differing Priorities

Whether the conflict is focused on the CRM implementation or a conflict pitting CRM priorities against something unrelated, being able to manage the varying priorities of your stakeholders on the project will be key to getting the appropriate level of participation from them. If individuals on the project team have differing project priorities, dealing with them from the very beginning of the project can be a big win.

Tools such as the project charter, project status discussion, and even design documents can be used to bring the team together and raise any important issues. If the conflict exists between CRM priorities and those associated with another organizational initiative, your executive sponsor and project steering committee are going to be the best mechanisms for you to resolve any problems. The larger your organization is, the more likely these types of conflicts are to occur. If necessary, plan to build some additional time into your project plan to account for small shifts in priorities throughout the project.

Application Adoption

We discussed application adoption earlier in this chapter. With that information in mind, all of the items outlined in this section of the chapter can contribute to a lack of application adoption. Having priorities that spread users too thin, over-scoping, a perception of lukewarm executive support, and other items should all be avoided where possible to allow users to adjust to the new application. Issues with application adoption could derail both your initial implementation and your ability to get support (and funding).

Addressing concerns quickly is important. Providing additional training, support time, and resources to your team throughout the process will enable the implementation to go well and should position your team well for any future phases.

Summary

Throughout this chapter, we have provided an overview of the different elements of your initial CRM project. Many of these topics could have a book dedicated to them alone, so we have provided what we feel is enough information to get you started and have some simple yet effective templates to work with. Based on our deep CRM consulting experience, we have also worked to identify some of the pitfalls associated with typical CRM implementations. When combined, it is our hope that this information gives you enough to ultimately be successful with the first step in your CRM program.

- Spending time up front in the project documenting the processes to be impacted by CRM will help align the team and result in a smoother project with fewer surprises.

- Formal use case development as part of the design stage can be helpful to both the design process and the subsequent testing effort.

- Custom development introduces risk to your project but can significantly increase the value of the application and its fit to your organization's processes.

- Data migration is a difficult and expensive task; limit it wherever feasible, and be realistic about its value.

- Integrating CRM with other business applications can set up employees to provide a better customer experience and make them more productive.

- Reporting is a key project element; consider the desired reporting outcomes at the beginning of the project and periodically throughout the design process to ensure that they will be delivered by the completed application.

CHAPTER 7

Maintaining and Evolving CRM

The previous chapters of this book provided the information you will need to successfully plan and launch your CRM program. In the long term, it is the continued maintenance and evolution, or *stewardship*, of CRM that will allow you to view your investment as worthwhile.

The goal of this chapter is to provide you with the necessary information to continue to evolve your CRM program following the initial deployment. Although we will talk about ongoing maintenance being paramount to long-term success, it is actually a combination of maintenance and the continued growth and progression of CRM that will allow you to clearly see success. The initial phase of a CRM implementation may go well, but without continued stewardship, the program will eventually cease to add value to your organization.

Role of the Steering Committee

Chapter 2 introduced the steering committee and its role in your CRM program. Although this group's role changes following the initial CRM deployment, the committee continues to remain of paramount importance to the long-term success of your CRM program. The steering committee needs to continue to act as the central point for all things CRM moving forward. Some ongoing focuses should include the following:

- *CRM evangelism*: The steering committee should plan to continue to act as the primary evangelist for the CRM program within your organization. Whether it is because of your need to secure funding for future phases and work or because of the importance of successful future projects to your organization, the message of success needs to be presented early and often. As such, it is important for the steering committee to tout the positives from the initial implementation and quickly address any negatives that arise. Finally, the steering committee can evangelize the organization's strategic CRM vision and articulate the business benefits of your CRM application.

- *Change control and roadmap planning and execution*: The steering committee is also the most appropriate mechanism for getting executives and decision makers into a room to make ongoing decisions. Although the group may not meet as frequently as during the initial CRM launch, having the executive audience available to make important decisions will allow future phases, quick fixes, and any issues to be addressed more quickly and efficiently.

- *Executive* support: Organizations generally experience varying levels of employee adoption when implementing a CRM program. Following the deployment, it is incumbent on the steering committee to ensure that people are using the processes and application as intended. This can typically be accomplished by an appropriate combination of "carrots" and "sticks" and will need to be specific to your organization. Some examples of possible incentives include the following:

  - Tying a portion of your sales reps' compensation to the information stored in their opportunities

  - Providing a bonus to your customer service team based on either customer satisfaction or whether they meet service level agreement (SLA) commitments to customers

  - Tracking conversion of leads to opportunities and providing the marketing team with incentive to assist with this conversion

Additionally, as you look to increase usage, gather feedback, or address any issues that arise, the steering committee can ensure that those responsible receive the proper time and response from employees. This will create an environment of collaboration within your organization.

Meeting Frequency

During the initial CRM implementation, the steering committee will meet frequently, often weekly, to ensure that the direction of the project is as expected. Immediately following the launch of CRM, it is still imperative for this schedule to continue. Too often, we see customers immediately drop the steering committee meetings a week or two after launch. In addition to providing a mechanism for issues to be quickly addressed by the senior leadership team associated with the project, the steering committee can act as a positive, unified voice during the critical time following launch.

As time goes on, the opportunity to reduce the frequency of these meetings exists. Within a couple weeks of launch, consider reducing the meetings to every other week. After approximately 60 days, begin to think about monthly discussions. Because a significant number of CRM implementations fail based on a lack of long-term follow-through and growth, it would not be wise to risk the long-term success of your CRM application; so, keep the steering committee involved, and continue these meetings.

Meeting Agenda

Like the frequency of the steering committee meetings, the discussion topics for these meetings change following launch. Much of the attention turns from managing the launch project team (internal or vendor) to ensuring employees are supported and planning for the next release.

The sample agenda in Figure 7-1 provides some guidance on the topics for post-deployment steering committee meetings. Although many of the items listed seem similar to implementation topics, you should still expect to assign things such as deliverables to people following launch. It is important to continually check on the status of these items to ensure the application is continuing to evolve.

Post Deployment – Sample Steering Committee Agenda

Meeting Date:

Meeting Attendees:

Meeting Location:

Agenda

1.   Overall Application Status

2.   Current Enhancement Schedule & Milestones

3.   Outstanding Deliverable

      3.1.   Deliverable Review

      3.2.   Status (% Complete)

4.   Resourcing

5.   Major Issues or Concerns Review

6.   Decision Requests

<This section of the document can be updated following the meeting to ensure all next steps were captured. It will also serve to remind team members of the next meeting.>

Post Meeting Notes / Updates

1.   Defined Action Items

      1.1.   TBD

      1.2.   TBD

2.   Next Meeting

Figure 7-1. Sample steering committee agenda

Meeting Attendees and Ownership

Following the initial deployment, a number of different individuals or roles will attend the steering committee meetings. This meeting will typically be attended by the following types of individuals:

- Initial project sponsor

- Departmental champions

- Support leads/team members providing support

- IT personnel monitoring/maintaining the CRM application

It is important to remember that the people in these roles during the initial implementation may change post-implementation. Additionally, as you roll out additional features of the CRM application or change processes during future releases, there may be others in your organization who should serve on the steering committee.

Maintaining CRM

Following the deployment of your CRM application, it is important that you quickly transition into maintenance mode. This phase of your project will revolve around providing needed support to users, triaging issues with the application, and ensuring that the key CRM documentation remains up to date.

Supporting Employees and Gathering Feedback

To keep CRM moving forward, it is important to provide an atmosphere where employees feel supported and issues don't fester. An organization's ability to address the inevitable questions and issues quickly will ultimately contribute greatly to CRM success and the ability to get resources, both financial and otherwise, to continue to grow the program.

One way to support employees is to identify specific champions who are both evangelists of the CRM program and know the CRM processes and application well enough to be experts around their specific use cases. The following are some examples of these people:

- *Stakeholders:* The stakeholders for the project are individuals who have a vested interest in the success of the project above and beyond that of the average employee. Project stakeholders should be prepared to serve as evangelists. Additionally, for many of the support and ongoing maintenance tasks, those specifically identified as stakeholders require more attention than others, given their importance to the overall program.

- *Departmental champions:* The departmental champion will provide overall guidance to the CRM team for a specific department's processes and CRM needs. This individual is often someone like a sales or service manager who may have the ear of the executive team. Some responsibilities of this individual are as follows:

    - Serve as an escalation point for any issues that arise post-launch

    - Contribute to on-going process and application design work

    - Serve as a functional expert on the application, helping support users within their business group, and if the application allows, make small modifications to the application required by users post-deployment

- *Project sponsor:* The project sponsor will provide overall guidance to the CRM team for a wide range of future phase initiatives. This individual is often a higher-level executive than any of those outlined thus far. Some responsibilities of this individual are as follows:

    - Provide executive guidance when dealing with the steering committee

    - Ensure that team members and other project stakeholders are available and provide design feedback as necessary

Identifying Issues

As part of the overall support of the implementation, being able to quickly identify and address any issues that arise is very important. Organizations should leverage their stakeholders and departmental champions to be their ears, listening for employees' issues. Listen for recurring questions, application usage problems, and water-cooler banter from employees to assist with identifying issues. Tracking issues as they arise may also assist with the identification of common problems. Being able to identify these issues and quickly react to them will help you prevent discontent from developing within your CRM community.

Providing Ongoing Support

As part of the launch process for your CRM program, either you or your selected vendor will provide CRM application support to end users for a short period of time. Simply because this period ends does not mean that the support for the application can end. Organizations should evaluate support options at their disposal to assist with providing this support moving forward.

Although it's sometimes overlooked, when they do provide long-term support, one mistake that organizations often make is providing support only for the technology and configurations deployed. It is highly likely that you will change your organization's processes during your CRM deployment, so ensuring that departmental champions and/or stakeholders are available to support any process questions that arise is also important.

Finally, encourage your application support staff to continually look deeper than the surface technology problem. Although a problem may be quickly solved by changing a setting or updating some data, viewing support in this way may cause you to overlook the root cause of the issue. The longer the root cause goes unaddressed, the more severe the impact once the issue is discovered.

In addition to leveraging an application to track issues, some other support mechanisms to consider are the following.

E-mail Feedback

Consider providing your user community with a way to submit feedback via e-mail. In addition to having a link to your CRM application, e-mail provides a quick and easy way for them to submit feedback via a tool that is familiar to them. Depending on the amount of controversy associated with your CRM program, accommodations can be made to allow employees to send anonymous e-mail as well.

To ensure the appropriate amount of information is received when feedback is provided, consider providing your users with a template like that shown in Figure 7-2 for issue submission.

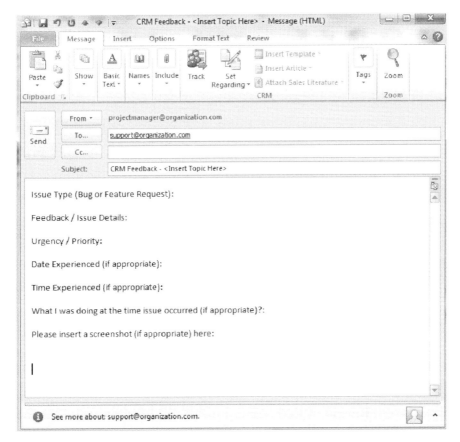

Figure 7-2. Support request e-mail template

The key point to highlight for employees is the importance of providing as much information as possible when outlining an issue. The more a support resource has to work with, the more likely they will be to solve the problem.

Centralized Feedback Capture

Another option for capturing and tracking feedback is to use a centralized location. Depending on the technical sophistication of your company, this could be as simple as a spreadsheet in a shared folder or as complex as a portal available inside and outside of the organization. Regardless of the approach taken, the information captured would be the same.

One distinct advantage to capturing issues and feedback this way is the transparency it provides users. Of course, this requires consistent updating and monitoring from the CRM team, but assuming that happens, users can continually feel invested in the process. Providing continual status updates may allow users to self-resolve some of their questions prior to reaching out to the team. Figure 7-3 shows a quick template for tracking feedback and issues raised by users.

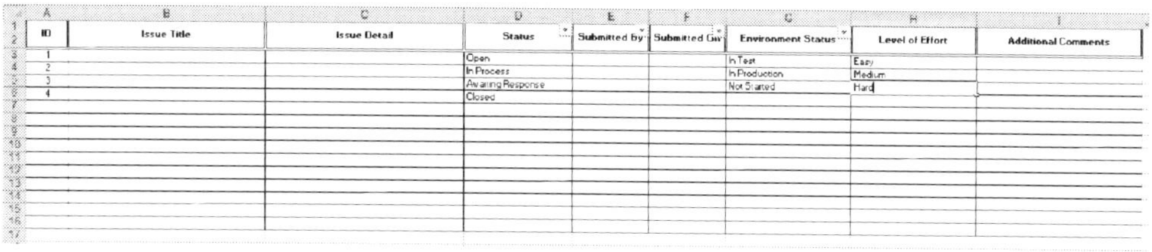

ID	Issue Title	Issue Detail	Status	Submitted By	Submitted [illegible]	Environment Status	Level of Effort	Additional Comments
1			Open			In Test	Easy	
2			In Process			In Production	Medium	
3			Awaiting Response			Not Started	Hard	
4			Closed					

Figure 7-3. Issue tracking list

Office Hours and Help Sessions

When deciding how to support your CRM community, a third component could be to set up "office hours" or scheduled help sessions. These types of sessions typically provide two significant values to your team:

- *Consistency*: Having regular office hours will provide your employees with a consistent support channel to which they can turn. Scheduling this time in advance will also provide users with the comfort of knowing that they have a defined, future time where support resources will be available to answer any questions or address concerns.

- *Randomness reduction*: One major implementation support danger is having the overall team become randomized by support requests. This will not only mean a reduction in the level or quality of support but may mean employees will feel neglected. By scheduling defined time, your employees can be trained to save requests for those scheduled times. Additionally, support resources can utilize this time to be focused on user concerns, whether that focus is on listening to them or addressing issues.

Updated Documentation

As employees settle in following your initial launch, leaving the CRM processes and application unchanged for a period will enable users to build up a familiarity and comfort with them. This comfort is key to user adoption and ultimately the launch's success.

During the time immediately following the launch, many small changes are likely to be made to the application. These changes will quickly address concerns that users have or small application bugs that were not caught during the testing phase of the application implementation. An often-overlooked task is updating the training documents and supporting resources to reflect these changes. The more up-to-date these documents are, the more likely your CRM community will be to utilize them as self-help resources as needed.

Once the dust has settled, you may have an opportunity to provide additional or enhanced documentation to the CRM community. This documentation can be set up to add value above and beyond the initial training guides. Although these new or enhanced documents may help your existing employees, they can also be used to support the ramp-up of new employees as they join the organization. Some examples of this documentation can include the following:

- *Training videos*: One way to augment the existing training materials available to employees is to begin developing a library of training videos. These videos can be two to five minutes in duration and can highlight a specific process or area of the CRM application.

- *Feature highlights*: Another option when trying to encourage growth of CRM within your organization is continually looking for small ways to provide additional value for the CRM community. One of way of doing this is to provide small snippets of information every week following deployment that highlight a new, often-overlooked, or small but powerful CRM application feature for users. In addition to keeping CRM top of mind across the organization, highlighting these features will provide instant, tangible value for those most heavily using the application day to day.

- *Usage success stories*: Although very similar to highlighting features within the application, outlining larger stories of success for employees may provide some added incentive to use CRM effectively. An example of these highlights might include a story about an instance where the CRM application enabled collaboration between teams or employees to achieve a desired result (a won sales opportunity, perhaps).

Tracking Feedback and Estimating Effort

As we have discussed, continually monitoring and tracking feedback from employees is very important. Being transparent about the feedback that has been received and how it is being addressed will provide your CRM community with a feeling of inclusion and should encourage them to continue to be actively involved in the CRM program.

In this section, we will provide information on what to do once feedback is received, as well as how to approach the estimation of effort associated with any required changes. The change control process is one that should be continuously running and could potentially have multiple iterations running at the same time.

Enhancing CRM

Once your application is launched and stable, and more specifically, support requests have slowed to a trickle, it is time to think about the next component of your CRM roadmap. Enhancements will enable you to continue to show progress to your user community to drive application adoption.

Change Control Process

The change control process is a continual process that helps organizations make changes and enhancements to their CRM program. Figure 7-4 shows how the process works.

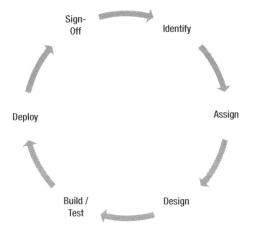

Figure 7-4. The change control process

The stages of the change control process are as follows:

- *Identify.* The identification phase of the change control process consists of identifying any changes or updates that need to be made to the CRM application or processes based on feedback from users. Although tracking this information is half the battle, understanding how the changes impact the program and, at a high level, understanding what will be required to make the changes is important. At this step in the process, a document should be used to clearly outline the update and the subsequent time or money needed to make it. Figure 7-5 shows an example document.

Change Request Overview

Briefly describe the change to the project. It should include how the change was requested or the need discovered.

1.   <Change Request Element #1>

    1.1.   Functional Overview

    1.2.   Scope Modificatoins

    1.3.   Key Assumptions

2.   <Change Request Element #2>

    2.1.   Functional Overview

    2.2.   Scope Modifications

    2.3.   Key Assumptions

3.   Impact of change

    It is helpful to describe the process used to identify the additional cost or schedule impacts. Ideally the process should be the same as the process used to estimate original project scope.

    3.1.   Budget Impact

Role	Hours
Project Manager	1
Developer	2
Analyst	3
TOTAL HOURS	6.0
TOTAL COST	$12,150

    3.2.   Schedule Impact

    3.3.   Project Risk Impact

Figure 7-5. Sample change request document

- *Assign*: During the assignment phase of the process, the steering committee will prioritize the change request document against other projects. Should the steering committee give priority to a specific item, it should be assigned to a resource to manage throughout the rest of the process. This doesn't necessarily have to be the person performing the work but rather the person who will ultimately ensure the work was completed. Some other items that should be considered during this phase of the process are as follows:

  - *Priority vs. other items*: What is this specific item's priority relative to others being proposed by the team? This is also a place where the steering committee's view of the overall organization will help in prioritizing CRM updates with other projects going on within the enterprise.

  - *Resourcing*: Changes to the CRM application can be handled by internal resources or can be outsourced to a vendor. It is the steering committee's responsibility to make this determination.

  - *Release timeline*: Once the priority and resourcing decisions have been made, a determination on release timeline can be evaluated. Often, considerations like busy seasons, quarter or fiscal year end, and other items could push companies to release items more or less quickly.

- *Design*: The design phase of the change control process is very similar to the design phase of the full CRM implementation. When scope items are implemented during the change control process, they are often much smaller in size than a full life-cycle project. As such, an abbreviated design phase can be considered. Design documentation may be nothing more than a brief functional specification and an outline of how the solution will be implemented. This level of detail will prevent copious amounts of time from being spent on small items but will ensure the design considers other important items that have been previously implemented.

- *Build/test (for application changes)*: Similar to the design phase, the build and test phase will often be slightly abbreviated. During the build portion of this phase, configuration changes will be made to CRM, and/or code will be written to address the requirement. During the test phase, the classic testing outlined in Chapter 6 should be completed. These types of testing include the following:

    - *Unit testing*: Unit testing includes a brief test of the configuration changes or developed components. Again, because of the nature of change request items, this testing is often completed quickly.

    - *System testing*: System testing includes an end-to-end review of the schema and user interface components. This allows the project developers and analysts to, for the first time, review how the changes will look when combined with other pieces of the application.

    - *Regression testing*: During the change control process, regression testing is the most important item to focus on. It enables the project team to test existing functionality to ensure that functionality didn't change during the latest release. Subsequent to each of the identified testing phases, regression testing should be completed. Not completing the appropriate amount of regression testing, and potentially introducing new issues into a stable CRM application, could cause distrust and longer-term issues for users.

- *Deploy*: The next stage of the change control process is deploying the change. In most cases, because of the smaller size of the change, this process is pretty simple and straightforward. It is the steering committee's responsibility at this point to ensure that the deployment of any changes doesn't conflict with other organizational project or priorities.

- *Signoff*: Once an item is deployed, it is critical to circle back with the steering committee and, if appropriate, the user who identified the original issue. As we have discussed a number of times, this effort will ensure that the process is correctly completed and will keep users engaged in the overall implementation.

Roadmap Development and Execution

Chapter 2 introduced the concept of a CRM roadmap, and Chapter 3 provided information on building this roadmap in order to align your organization's business objectives with your CRM program. As you identify new CRM processes or new CRM application features, it is important to keep this roadmap in sight at all times. Based on the agility of your organization, you may consciously add or adjust roadmap initiatives as you move through the process, but using the roadmap as a guide during those discussions will ensure you keep heading toward what you've previously defined as end state success. The following example provides one example of how you might address an initiative in your roadmap and, ultimately, how your organization's processes and application may change.

Example

Your company has been using CRM for two years and has followed the change control process we have outlined in this chapter. As part of a growth spurt within your industry, you decide to acquire another company. This company is located in a market that is different from your current location. There are a number of questions you must answer as you evaluate how your CRM application should change as a result of this acquisition.

Application-Specific Questions

Because of the new office location for your company, you need to gauge the impact on your CRM application. The following are some important questions:

- How will this new office impact the way users access the application? Has your organization always provided remote access to users, or will we need to evaluate that?

- Are there any local customs or rules that will impact how we utilize CRM? Do we need to include additional language in our quote and order documentation?

- Will the organization need to run different reports given the new location?

Once you answer these types of questions, you may be able to make application-specific updates to accommodate this new user community.

Process-Specific Questions

In addition to updating CRM, you may also need to consider updating CRM processes across your organization. The following are some valuable questions to ask:

- How will you onboard the new sales team into our CRM tool? What training should occur?

- Does the acquired company have any unique sales processes that must be considered as we bring them into the fold? Is there an opportunity for your existing sales team to learn from their sales model?

- Are there process or automation updates we can make that will enable a more seamless sales process regardless of geographical difference?

Ultimately, it is important to take both application and process changes into account when working through an initiative from your roadmap. In addition to handling these individual initiatives, your business environment may change as your company grows, the economy shifts, or you look to take advantage of opportunities in your market. There is nothing wrong with taking advantage of these situations, especially as it relates to your CRM environment, but it places even more importance on reviewing and consistently updating your CRM roadmap.

With this in mind, although much of the change control process identified earlier in this chapter focuses on managing changes to CRM following your initial deployment, there is a similar yet distinctly different process for managing the larger enhancements associated with executing your roadmap. This section will focus on differences between the initial project implementation process and the process for subsequent projects.

Managing Large Application Enhancements

Earlier this chapter, we identified the process for managing enhancements. That process is still valid when managing larger items as well. Figure 7-6 shows two small additions to the tracking spreadsheet: a "Type" column and "Risk" column; these will help you differentiate those items that can be deployed quickly and as interim items from those that require a large-scale deployment or new phase.

Figure 7-6. Issues list + Type and Risk columns

Large enhancements also require significantly more planning than quick fixes. Although you may release quick fixes on a relatively rapid cadence and may complete most small updates using internal resources, significantly more thought should go into larger, new-phase items and upgrades.

Scheduling Deployments

The scheduling considerations associated with a new project or an upgrade are much more significant than those associated with small, quick updates. The risk of creating unnecessary churn, bugs, or general concern by the user community is significantly higher the larger the project or upgrade.

The following are some important scheduling considerations:

- Impact on users:

  - What is the impact of the consolidated list of changes on your current user community?

  - Will users' existing processes or use cases change dramatically?

  - Are users still struggling with effectively using the initial deployment?

These are all important questions to consider. If the impact to user is significant, you may want to be more conscious of other things happening in the organization such as quarter ends, high support volumes, and so on. If the processes modeled in the application will change dramatically, it may be important to allow for additional user acceptance test or training time. Finally, if users are still struggling with using the initial deployment consistently, it may make sense to hold off on a second project until usage as stabilized.

- *Effort*: There are different levels of effort that will be associated with a future phase or upgrade. Much like the initial implementation, the effort associated with a follow-on project can vary greatly. This effort is also going to vary from that associated with an upgrade, because the tasks and focuses will be completely different. These differences will be outlined later in this chapter.

- *Risks*: A number of factors can contribute to the risk determination during a follow-on project or upgrade deployment. Some of those factors include the following:

  - *Number of scope items*: Typically, the larger the number of scope items, the larger the risk. Although this is not always the case, a bigger scope means more to manage, more to test, and more places bugs can be inserted into the deployment process.

- *Timing of deployment.* The timing of the deployment is important when evaluating risk. Poor timing could mean that users focus less attention on the design, a struggle focusing on user acceptance testing, or may cause users to quickly forget what is taught in training because of other priorities.

- *Product version longevity.* This is more of a concern with upgrades but should be considered for any future phases. The length of time a product version has been available also impacts the potential pitfalls that will exist for users and the amount of testing that needs to be done prior to deployment.

Resources: Vendor vs. Internal

As discussed in Chapter 4, quite a few decisions go into selecting the resources that will complete most of the work, typically a vendor, during the initial implementation. Many of those criteria should continue to be evaluated as you look at a future phase or upgrade. Some additional considerations are as follows:

- *Who is the correct vendor?* Many of the criteria that you used to evaluate vendors initially still apply during a follow-on project or an upgrade. That said, there are two more important questions:

  - Which vendor is more likely to be able to work with your team? Now that your team has been educated and has worked with the application for a period of time, which vendor is more likely to be a partner in the implementation process as opposed to needing to own the whole implementation? Some vendors are more likely to be able to support smaller, part-time implementations, while others are more comfortable with larger, full-time, multi-member teams. Please note, should you decide to switch vendors between initial and follow-on projects, you should allow for some additional time and budget for design changes. A new vendor will bring new ideas or a streamlined approach to an existing process or application.

- *How much work should the internal team do?* Now that your team has learned during phase 1 and has worked with the application following the initial deployment, how much work should the team do during the next phase or upgrade? Part of the answer will depend on the knowledge and skills of the internal implementation team. Overall, your team should be more capable of owning work and should feel comfortable teaming with vendors during future phases.

Testing

The number of features typically included in a follow-on project or a new version of a CRM application, combined with potential impact on the existing user community, means testing takes on additional importance. Although the classic testing approaches should all be completed, regression testing becomes more and more important the further away you are from the original deployment.

When performing testing during a follow-up implementation, regardless of which type of testing is occurring, it's important to do four things:

- Review previous test plans used for other phases and quick fixes.

- Develop detailed regression test plans to effectively test old functionality, new functionality, and the bridge between the two.

- Ensure significant time is dedicated to user acceptance testing. Users will frequently notice issues with the application before the project team providing users with an extended period (two or three weeks) to test the old and new features on your environment.

- Following the testing sessions, allow for time to fix or update the application.

Internal Release Management

Managing the release of new features and new versions requires a lot of forethought. As a steering committee or team leading the deployment, there are typically two categories of release management activities:

- *Infrastructure migration/release management*: Most follow-on phases and upgrades will include the setup or development and/or test environments. As part of the release, it will be imperative for someone to manage the promotion of code and customizations between these environments.

- *New feature/process release management:* Inevitably, when large sets of features or a new application version are released, the processes that users follow when interacting with the application will change. Ensuring users have time to digest these process changes, update their usage scenarios, and have any questions answered will go a long way toward ensuring a smooth transition to the new version or set of features.

When managing the overall release, two types of documents can be used in conjunction to help track the associated tasks. Figure 7-7 is a checklist that can be used to identify needed tasks during the go-live process. This checklist can be referred to at any point leading up to or during the actual deployment.

CRM
Go-Live Checklist

Task	Assigned To	Required Completion Date	Completion Date	Completed By
Pre-Deployment Activities				
Database Backups	Bob	6/1/11	6/1/11	Bob
Document Cutover Plan	Tom	6/1/11		
Deployment Activities				
Add New Users	Tom	6/2/11		
Prepare Email Communications	Jane	6/3/11		
Post-Deployment Activities				
Update Training Material Screenshots	Jane	6/1/11		

Figure 7-7. CRM go-live checklist example

In addition to this document, we have found a step-by-step guide to the release process to be a helpful tool when trying to avoid any last-minute issues. Although it is unlikely that any document will capture every issue, a carefully generated document, with screenshots and detailed steps, will help put the deployment team at ease. Figure 7-8 is a sample table of contents from a document like this.

CONTENTS

I. CRM ARCHITECTURE 3

1.0 SERVERS 3

1.1 DISK SPACE AND PRE-DEPLOYMENT SOFTWARE VERSIONS 3

II. SCHEDULED CRM DEPLOYMENTS 4

2.0 BACKUP PLAN 4

2.1 RESTORE PLAN 4

2.2 EXPORTING/IMPORTING CUSTOMIZATIONS 4

2.3 DEPLOYMENT ACTIVITIES 4

2.4 POST DEPLOYMENT ACTIVITIES 4

III. 3RD PARTY PRODUCTS 5

IV. CRM REPORT DEPLOYMENT PROCESS 6

V. POST DEPLOYMENT TESTING 7

5.1 SYSTEM TESTING 7

5.2 REGRESSION TESTING 7

5.3 USER ACCEPTANCE TESTING 7

VI. DEPLOYMENT COMMUNICATIONS 8

***Figure 7-8.** Deployment step-by-step guide*

Please note that the specific content of this document will vary depending on your CRM hosting situation. If you rely upon a vendor to host the application, many of the backup and restore activities become their responsibility to complete. Additionally, the process for deploying things such as reports may change depending on where the servers and application reside, but a plan to ensure they're appropriately deployed and testing is important. Again, where time permits, having step-by-step instructions with screenshots will alleviate issues during the deployment process.

New Application Versions and Upgrades

Throughout this chapter, we have discussed the role of the steering committee and how to handle new phases and deployments. The concepts we've outlined around managing releases and deploying new functionality are valid regardless of whether you're deploying new functionality on the same version of the application or are preparing your team for a version upgrade.

In this section, we will provide some specific guidance and information on things to expect when focusing specifically on an upgrade.

Cloud-Based Applications

If you are utilizing a hosted CRM application, your upgrade process will vary greatly from that of an on-premise instance of CRM. Depending on your hosting approach, you will have some different decisions to make, and the process will be slightly different, but ultimately, the responsibility for the upgrade process will fall mostly on the hosting vendor. Some specific differences are as follows:

- *Vendor-hosted CRM*: If you chose the vendor-hosted model earlier in the process, there is very little that you'll have to do as part of an upgrade. In general, most hosting vendors will provide an upgrade schedule or date where your instance of CRM will be upgraded. You will primarily be responsible for managing any updates or changes to installed clients in your enterprise. Depending on the hosting vendor, it may be prudent to at least understand their backup procedures in case the upgrade was to fail, but the credible CRM vendors have this process completely figured out.

- *Co-located CRM*: If you chose the co-location model when selecting your CRM application, there is likely some gray area associated with an upgrade. Depending on your hosting agreement with the vendor, you may or may not be responsible for executing the upgrade. If you are responsible, the release management process, testing, and so on, outlined earlier in this chapter will be important for you to follow. If the co-location hosting vendor is responsible for your upgrade, asking questions around backup and restore procedures, necessary infrastructure upgrades, and new client installations will ensure all your bases are covered.

On-Premises Applications

For on-premises applications, the upgrade process is similar to the decision and release management process outlined previously in this chapter. You can essentially treat this new version as a future phase of the implementation. The one major consideration with upgrades that isn't present with new features is the necessity of infrastructure upgrades. Depending on the release frequency of your CRM application's new version, new versions of the database software, operating system, or client software may be needed for your application to work appropriately. Should any of these items need to be upgraded alongside the CRM application, additional planning, testing, and documentation will be necessary to ensure a successful migration.

Application Betas

Many CRM vendors will also offer beta access to their new CRM releases. There are some advantages and disadvantages to implementing a beta application.

Here are the advantages:

- Frequently, being a beta participant comes with some advantages to the customer. Whether this advantage is a short-term deal on license or hosting costs or some publicity associated with being a beta customer, you should expect some value from implementing prerelease software.

- By utilizing beta software, you will have access to the new features before other customers. Depending on the features and their importance to your organization, having access to using them may add value to your user community and/or solve an existing challenge being experienced by your organization.

Here are the disadvantages:

- Depending on your hosting decision, there may be some additional pain associated with implementing beta software. The earlier you participate in the beta process, the more likely you are to have to reinstall the application when the application becomes generally available to other customers.

- If your organization is not technologically sophisticated, the issues associated with implementing software that inherently contains bugs and the angst they will cause your user community may not be worth the benefits.

- Features you may find useful or plan to customize may be cut from the final version of the software.

Monitoring the Vendor Ecosystem

Regardless of whether you have just completed your initial deployment or you are a number of phases or upgrades into your CRM journey, it is important to keep an eye on the vendor ecosystem associated with your specific CRM application. In this section of the chapter, we will provide some high-level information on the various ways you can monitor what is happening around your tool.

Conferences

Many larger CRM vendors have an annual conference. Making the investment to send someone from your organization to these events could inform you of new application features that are important to your organization.

These conferences typically include a functional track that could be beneficial for your SMEs, project sponsor, or departmental champions. As members of the steering committee, understanding what is available in upcoming releases will help you prioritize development efforts and assist in managing releases.

Most conferences also include a more technically focused track. These tracks are a great way to get your internal team further ramped up on the CRM technology. Participating in the technical track sessions, many of which include hands-on labs, will allow your internal team to ask questions of product experts and learn to perform more implementation tasks themselves.

New Independent Software Vendors (ISVs)

As CRM vendors continue to grow their products, CRM users need to continue to monitor the ISV landscape. ISVs present a buy vs. build option to customers when new features are needed. Understanding your ISV options when planning to roll out a new feature will enable you to make the most informed decision.

The other consistent change in the ISV community relates to upgrades from product vendors. A primary goal of product vendors is to continually provide features to customers that are in high demand. Fundamentally, this goal conflicts with that of ISVs; they are motivated to fill holes in the application as they are discovered by customers. Naturally then, as CRM vendors release new versions of their applications with features that are similar to the ISV's products, ISVs must adapt and create new products or add substantially better features to existing ones.

User Groups

If your organization is in a larger metropolitan area, you may also be able to participate in user groups sponsored by or focused around your CRM product. Like conferences, there are a number of benefits associated with participating in user groups. As we previously mentioned, staying on top of changes to the ISV community will help you as you expand CRM usage through your organization. Oftentimes, ISVs will participate as presenters in user groups, enabling you to get a quick, low-pressure look at new ISV products on the market.

The other big advantage to user group attendance is an opportunity to speak with other peers about how they are using their CRM application to solve problems. You may be working through a similar business problem as another, noncompetitive company, so being able to have an open forum for discussion could suggest easier, more cost-effective solutions to the business problems you're trying to address.

Blogs and Newsletters

Many product vendors and consultants produce blog postings and newsletters that address questions or issues frequently encountered in their respective applications. These two items will also likely have different focuses from your perspective, so having someone in your organization viewing both is important.

- *Blogs*: Employees from product vendors and consultants will often produce blog postings on a regular basis. Because most are biased toward their respective products, they tend to be specific in nature. That said, generic blogs on solving business problems with CRM do exist and approach these challenges in a technology-agnostic way. Blog postings are rarely broad but are specific in nature and either functionally focused or technically focused, but not both.

- *Newsletters*: Consultants tend to be more proactive in providing newsletters than product vendors. Newsletter content is often consciously broad and will appeal to a wide audience.

Consultants

As we discussed in Chapter 4, a number of criteria can be used to evaluate and select your CRM consultants. After completing the initial phase of your deployment, you will obviously have a better feel for the vendor you chose, as well as the things you'd like to look for in the vendor used for future phases.

As we discussed earlier this chapter, you may also want to look for different features in your sustainment vendor than you would in the vendor used during phase 1. As your team grows their skills, you may find that you need less time from vendors, so finding a vendor with a flexible support and engagement model will enable you to save money while continuing to receive the best service.

Finally, much like those in the ISV channel, vendors are consistently changing their offerings and focuses. By reviewing their blog and newsletters and staying engaged with them periodically during times when you are not heavily utilizing their services, you will be able to quickly engage with the appropriate consultant when you decide to undertake additional work.

Final Thoughts on Maintaining and Evolving CRM

Throughout this chapter, we have discussed the items for you to focus on following the initial launch of your CRM program. Placing a priority on these items, while consistently keeping your CRM roadmap in mind, will enable you to grow and expand usage of CRM within your organization. Post-launch, virtually everything you do will have an impact on the CRM community, so a defined testing process, a plan associated with new features and projects, and a focus on listening to and supporting your employees will enable you to continue your progress and, ultimately, achieve success with your CRM program.

Conclusion

Ideally you are finishing this book with a feeling of confidence and optimism about your ability to start, manage, and grow your organization's CRM program. Our intent has been to break down this potentially daunting task into its component parts, describe each in detail, and leave you with a sense of how they all fit together. CRM is not rocket science, but it requires diligence and energy and thoughtfulness; you and your organization will get from it what you put into it.

In wrapping up, we would like to leave you with a few last pieces of advice: what we would consider the "big picture" takeaways for CRM success, more important than any application feature or document template we have provided.

Communication

Work to establish open and regular dialogue with all the CRM stakeholders, including senior executives, CRM application users, the CRM administration team, IT representatives, managers, and so on. This is critical to spot issues that can impact the program early, to identify opportunities for improvement, and to make sure that the key people in your organization remain supporters of the CRM program. Different stakeholder groups may prefer different formats; for senior executives, a regular lunch meeting might be appropriate, where for end users, some kind of regular CRM "office hours" session could be the best way to connect. The point is, find a way to meaningfully engage with all of the CRM stakeholder groups regularly.

Be a Cheerleader for CRM

Especially when establishing a new CRM program, frequent, vocal support for CRM is important. In communications with the organization, continue to tout the importance of CRM to your mission and organization goals, and look for opportunities to highlight both the employees making great contributions to the program, and the tangible results of the organization's investment in CRM.

Monitor CRM Application Usage

If a particular group or key user's activity in the CRM application falls off, this is an important red flag that should be investigated. It could indicate that a group's processes have changed and the CRM application no longer cleanly supports them. When this happens, users begin to develop their own tools and workarounds outside the CRM application, and application usage declines.

Use Technology to Solve Real Problems

When plotting the roadmap for your CRM program, it may be tempting to allow the application to lead the way, focusing on new application features and add-ons, and then trying to find a place in the organization where they add value to justify a position for them on the roadmap. This is the tail wagging the dog. Be watchful for this kind of thinking creeping into your project team. Focus on the challenges and opportunities faced by the organization. First understand the business problems, and then begin your search for a solution. We aren't suggesting you remain ignorant of new application capabilities, only that you focus on the business needs first. Technology is worse than useless if it does not solve a problem that your organization cares about.

This same theme crops up throughout your CRM program in application design and in report design, so maintain a focus on solving real problems and don't deploy technology just because it's there. A plethora of unused application features and flashy dashboards serve only to confuse users and distract them from the work they need to accomplish. Make sure everything you put in front of users is of value to the organization.

Tailor Our Guidance to Your Organization

The content of this book is based on our experience working with many organizations on establishing and growing successful CRM programs, but as with most things, there is no one-size-fits-all approach to CRM. If you attempt to rigidly apply the approaches outlined in this book word for word, you may struggle. Understand how your organization operates, and use your judgment to apply the guidance in this book to your own situation.

Index

▓ K

KPIs and compensation to CRM usage, 148

▓ L

Lack of executive support, 151
Launching solution, cutover, 144
    client application installation, 145–146
    final data migration, 145
    post-deployment support, 147–148
    user communications, 146–147
Linking data between systems, 116

▓ M, N

Maintaining and evolving CRM, 153, 173
    application support, 157
        centralized feedback capture, 158
        e-mail feedback, 157
        office hours and help sessions, 159
    departmental champions, 156
    effort estimation, 160
    grow and expand usage
        cheerleaders, 173
        communication, 173
        guidance, 174
        monitoring application usage, 173
        technology to solve problems, 174
    identifying issues, 157
    monitoring vendor ecosystem, *See*
        Monitoring vendor ecosystem
    project sponsor, 157
    stakeholders, 156
    steering committee, *See* Steering committee
    tracking feedback, 160
    updated documentation, 159
        feature highlights, 160
        training videos, 160
        usage success stories, 160
Managing data-level integration, 114
    data mapping, 115
    identify integration scenarios and
        applications, 114
Managing differing priorities, 151–152
Managing user interface integration, 116
Mock migration testing, 131
    guidelines, 131
    validation, 131
    query testing, 132
    review error logs, 131
    spot testing, 132
Monitoring vendor ecosystem
    blogs and newsletters, 172
    conferences, 171
    consultants, 172
    ISVs, 171–172
    user groups, 172

▓ O

Organization's "as is" process definition, 101–102
Organization's "to be" process definition, 102–103
Overly complicated design, 150–151
Over-scoping, 150

▓ P

People management, 149
Performance testing, 134
Pick-list mapping, 129–130
Planning data migration, 132
    schedule, 132–133
    script, 133
Post-deployment support, 147–148
Presentation reporting tools, 121
Professional services agreement (PSA), 93
Purpose-built application data migration tools, 130–131

▓ Q

Quality of data, 125, 126
Query testing, 132

▓ R

Red flags
    designing projects
        business impact, 40
        by business process, 41
        by department, 40
        by duration/effort, 41
        by geography, 41
        outcomes, 41
    Ideashare, *See* Ideashare

▒ S

2462540R00132

Printed in Great Britain
by Amazon.co.uk, Ltd.,
Marston Gate.